IT HAPPENED IN
TENNESSEE

It Happened In Series

IT HAPPENED IN
TENNESSEE

Susan Sawyer

TWODOT®

GUILFORD, CONNECTICUT
HELENA, MONTANA

AN IMPRINT OF THE GLOBE PEQUOT PRESS

A · TWODOT® · BOOK

The publisher gratefully acknowledges the assistance of Michael E. Birdwell, Assistant Professor of History at Tennessee Technological University.

Cover art © 2002 by Lisa Harvey, Helena, Montana.

Sawyer, Susan.
It happened in Tennessee/Susan Sawyer.
   p. cm.—(It happened in series)
Includes bibliographical references and index.
   1. Tennessee—History—Anecdotes. I. Title. II. Series.
F436.6S25 2002
976.8—dc21   2002021513
ISBN: 0-7627-1164-7

Manufactured in the United States of America

First Edition/Fourth Printing

Contents

Preface

As a native and resident of Tennessee, I'm quite proud to hail from the Volunteer State. Researching this book, I've uncovered dozens of fascinating events that have shaped and molded the course of my home state's history. This book spotlights thirty events from Tennessee's rich and colorful past.

The stories in this book do not offer a complete history of the state. Instead they uncover some lesser known historical events and offer behind-the-scenes information on several famous happenings. On the following pages you'll find stories about well-known personalities from Tennessee, ranging from the hot-headed Andrew Jackson to the one-and-only Elvis Presley. You'll find heartbreaking stories about the tragic loss of life during events such as yellow fever epidemics and Civil War battles. And you'll find inspirational stories on topics ranging from baseball to television movies.

Each story offers a complete glimpse into one event from Tennessee's history. You can choose to read the chapters out of sequence, or read the book straight through. But no matter how you choose to read this book, I hope you'll gain a new appreciation for the rich and colorful history of the wonderful state of Tennessee!

—Susan Sawyer
Chattanooga, Tennesee

The Transylvania Purchase

· 1775 ·

It was a land deal that has never been matched, marking the largest real estate transaction in American history. On March 14, 1775, the Cherokee exchanged over two million acres of land for a few thousand pounds of goods and sterling. The transaction took place at Sycamore Shoals, in the area now known as Elizabethton, Tennessee.

The man primarily responsible for the incredible business deal was Richard Henderson, an ambitious land speculator and associate justice of the North Carolina supreme court. Eager to reap vast financial rewards from buying and developing western lands, Henderson hired an agent to explore the uncharted lands west of the Appalachian mountain range. Henderson's agent, Daniel Boone, led the way to the Kentucky River, blazing new trails into the untamed wilderness. Henderson soon followed Boone over the newly created Wilderness Road with additional settlers.

Henderson hoped to transform the region, known as Transylvania, into a proprietary colony similar to Pennsylvania and Maryland. His judicial position, however, prevented him from taking an active role in land speculation until the expiration of his term in 1774. He then formed the Louisa Land Company, quickly reorganizing the business under the name of the

Transylvania Company in 1775. Within a short time, Henderson, along with his partner, Nathaniel Hart, and agent Boone, traveled to the Overhill region of the Cherokee Nation to negotiate the purchase of Cherokee lands. To sweeten his prospects of success, Henderson assembled six wagons of goods that he hoped to use in making a profitable deal with the tribe.

Henderson and his associates invited Cherokee leaders to meet with them for talks at Sycamore Shoals in the Watauga settlement on March 1, 1775. Formed in 1772, Watauga was the first permanent American settlement outside of the original thirteen colonies. Most people believe that the settlement also established the first majority rule system of American democratic government.

Cherokee began to gather at Sycamore Shoals as early as January, apparently curious about the pending offer by the Transylvania Company. Henderson arranged for the Watauga settlers to provide food for the Cherokee during their visit. Word of the upcoming negotiations spread through the Overhill region, and over twelve hundred Cherokees and six hundred settlers had gathered at Sycamore Shoals by March 1.

After two weeks of bargaining, the Cherokee agreed to exchange more than twenty million acres of land for approximately eight thousand pounds of goods and two thousand pounds sterling. The purchase included much of what is now Middle Tennessee and about two-thirds of Kentucky. Before leaving the bargaining table, Henderson also purchased a "path deed" for an additional two thousand pounds sterling, gaining access to his lands through the Cumberland Gap.

After three Cherokee chiefs, Attakullakulla, Ocanastota, and Savanook, signed the agreement on March 19, 1775, the deed for the Transylvania Purchase was recorded in the Hawkins County Register of Deeds Office in Rogersville. Many deeds transferring land from the Transylvania Company to new owners were later recorded in Rogersville.

Some Cherokee leaders were not pleased with the deal,

particularly Chief Attakullakulla's nephew, Dragging Canoe. After the Cherokee concluded the conference with the white settlers, Dragging Canoe pointed north and warned that the area would become "a dark and bloody ground." Determined to drive the settlers from Cherokee lands, Dragging Canoe and several young Creek and Cherokee warriors formed the Chickamauga confederation and proceeded to lead violent attacks on white settlements. Fort Watauga near Sycamore Shoals became a refuge for settlers in need of protection from the Indians.

Legal problems plagued the transaction, as well. Although a provisional, democratic government for the Transylvania region was organized in May 1775, the Continental Congress ignored Transylvania's plea to be recognized as the fourteenth colony. To make matters worse, the project did not meet with British approval under the Royal Proclamation of 1763, which denounced further white settlement on Cherokee lands. Moreover, the chartered limits of Transylvania encompassed Virginia and North Carolina lands. By the time Virginia and North Carolina attained statehood, both states had voided the Transylvania Company's land titles.

In compensation for their labor and expenses in promoting western colonization, Henderson and his associates were awarded two hundred thousand acres of land from both Virginia and North Carolina. Although the leaders of the Transylvania Company eventually received only a small portion of the vast territory that they had originally acquired from the Cherokee, the Transylvania Purchase played a strategic role in the early days of the western frontier by opening the door for further expansion.

The Lost State of Franklin

• 1784 •

In the decade before Tennessee obtained statehood in 1796, a group of settlers from the region nearly changed the course of the state's history. In 1784, four counties created an independent state known as Franklin—and almost succeeded in gaining the approval of the Continental Congress to admit Franklin as the fourteenth state in the union.

During the early 1780s, settlers in the area west of the Appalachian mountain range became increasingly dissatisfied with the state and federal governments' ability to protect them from Indian attacks. At the time, the Mississippi River served as the western boundary of North Carolina, and residents of the western portion of the state felt slighted by and isolated from state government. No state courts existed west of the Appalachians, and new inhabitants desperately needed one to record land deeds in the region. By 1784, a group of settlers had decided to form a new, independent state that would meet their pressing needs. They turned to a prominent veteran of the Revolutionary War, John Sevier, for leadership in forming the new state.

On August 23, 1784, Sevier gathered with a group of settlers in a log courthouse in Jonesboro to plan an independent state. The group decided to name the new state in honor of statesman Benjamin Franklin. Sevier agreed to serve as governor of Franklin, which consisted of the four counties of Washington, Sullivan, Greene, and Hawkins. Hawkins County was later subdivided to include the counties of Wayne, Caswell, Spencer, Sevier, and Blount.

By 1785, the Franklinites had drawn up a state constitution and designated Jonesboro as the state capital. Taxes were levied, laws were passed, and Franklin functioned in the same manner as any other state. But North Carolina failed to recognize Franklin's statehood. Instead of acknowledging the state of Franklin, the North Carolina General Assembly assumed the role of a forgiving parent by passing an act to pardon Franklinites for their roles in separating the lands that made up Franklin from North Carolina

But Governor Sevier and his followers responded by appealing to a higher authority: the Continental Congress. After an unsuccessful attempt to win North Carolina's approval, Franklin sent delegate William Cocke to New York to petition the Continental Congress for statehood. Statesman Thomas Jefferson favored the petition, predicting that Franklin would win statehood from North Carolina. Benjamin Franklin, however, offered little support for Franklin's admission as the fourteenth state. After Cocke informed Franklin that the leaders of the independent state wished to name the state in his honor, Franklin replied that he was flattered, but offered no assistance and declined an invitation to visit the area.

As delegates to the Continental Congress considered the Franklin petition, North Carolina abstained from voting. Under the law, admission into the union required approval by two-thirds of the states, requiring nine votes from the thirteen states. After the votes were cast, the final count revealed seven ayes—two short of the required votes for passage.

Although Franklin continued to operate as an independent state, problems plagued the region. Still claiming Franklin as its own, North Carolina labeled the Franklin area as Washington County, North Carolina, and set up a government for the area.

North Carolina designated Greensboro as the new state capital, replacing Jonesboro. Bitter competition between the two governments resulted in courthouse raids, with each party stealing the other's records. Moreover, the instability of Franklin's currency forced the independent state to pay its public servants in furs instead of money. Governor Sevier received one thousand deerskins as his annual salary, while the state's chief justice received five hundred deerskins. Five hundred raccoon skins served as payment to the governor's secretary, and the justice of the peace received one muskrat skin for each signed warrant.

Franklin's population peaked about 1788, with some forty thousand residents. Although the king of Spain offered to provide protection for the state in exchange for oaths of allegiance from Franklinites, Governor Sevier declined the offer. Lured by stories of rich lands in the west, residents of Franklin began leaving the area in the late 1780s. The decline of Franklin continued as the federal government signed the Treaty of Hopewell with the Cherokee, turning over a large portion of the state to the Indians, including the capital of Greensboro.

Unable to survive on its own, the state of Franklin disappeared in 1789. No one replaced the state's governor at the end of his four-year term. Sevier was elected to serve as Washington County's senator for the state of North Carolina and appointed brigadier general of the Washington County militia, and the state resumed rule over the Franklin region. When the lands west of the Appalachians gained admission to the union as the state of Tennessee in 1796, Sevier was inaugurated as Tennessee's first governor.

By the time Tennessee became the nation's sixteenth state, the state of Franklin was all but forgotten. Today, few Tennesseans realize how close they came to becoming known as Franklinites. According to one historian, "The situation was one without parallel in American jurisprudence, since Franklin was and is the only example of a de facto American state that functioned in every aspect of [state] power."

Andrew Jackson's Duel

• 1806 •

Long before his rise to fame as a military leader and the seventh president of the United States, Andrew Jackson was known for his aggressive, forceful personality. Never one to back down from a challenge, he honored and accepted the code of dueling as a method of settling disputes between gentlemen. To resolve months of heated disagreements with attorney Charles Dickinson, Jackson took part in a memorable duel on a fateful May morning in 1806.

Conflicts between the two Tennesseans erupted late in 1805, when Jackson received word that Dickinson had spoken unfavorably about Jackson's wife, Rachel. When Jackson married Rachel Donelson in 1791, her divorce from her first husband had not yet been finalized. Any talk of the scandalous situation enraged Jackson, who adamantly vowed that he would never allow anyone to mar his wife's name. True to his word, Jackson confronted Dickinson, claiming he had taken Rachel's "sacred name" into his "polluted mouth." Although the Nashville attorney insisted he must have been drunk at the time, he apologized for making such remarks. Jackson accepted the apology and went on his way.

But a dispute over a horserace soon deepened the hostilities between the two men. Socially prominent in Nashville, Dickinson was the leader of a group of carefree young men who enjoyed horseracing. One member of the group, Joseph Ervin, entered his horse in a race against Jackson's prized stallion. Before the start of the race, however, Ervin was forced to pull the horse from the race and pay a forfeiture fee to Jackson. Although Jackson accepted Ervin's notes, Dickinson and Jackson later disagreed over the payment.

The dispute led to additional quarrels between Jackson's and Dickinson's friends, including Thomas Swann. When Jackson referred to Swann as a "damned liar," Swann promptly demanded a duel. Jackson refused, insisting that Swann was not a gentleman worthy of a duel, but a boy who deserved a caning. Later, during an encounter with Swann in a local tavern, Jackson struck the young man with his cane. In retaliation, Swann publicly denounced Jackson by writing scathing letters about the situation to Nashville's only newspaper, the *Impartial Review and Cumberland Repository*.

Dickinson quickly leaped to the defense of his friends. Penning a letter to the *Review*, he wrote, "I declare [Andrew Jackson] to be a worthless scoundrel, 'a poltroon and coward'—a man who, by frivolous and evasive pretexts, avoided giving the satisfaction which was due to a gentleman whom he had injured."

Realizing that Dickinson was the leader of the group, Jackson challenged him to a duel. Embracing the formal tone associated with dueling, he wrote: "Your conduct and expressions relative to me of late have been of such a nature and so insulting that it requires and shall have my notice. . . . I hope, Sir, your courage will be ample security to me that I may obtain speedily that satisfaction due me for insults offered."

Dickinson promptly accepted the challenge. Close friends of the two men arranged the details of the upcoming duel, choosing a small field located across the state border in Kentucky as the site of the showdown. As word spread of the scheduled match, observers placed bets on the outcome, favoring Dickinson's superior marksmanship. Widely regarded as the best marksman in the state, Dickinson constantly practiced with his pistols.

By the time the two men arrived at the dueling grounds on the morning of May 30, 1806, both Jackson and Dickinson had carefully planned their strategies. Confident of his speed and accuracy with a pistol, Dickinson wagered that he would strike a particular button on Jackson's jacket. Aware that Dickinson would almost certainly hit him before he could fire, Jackson was determined to take his opponent's first bullet. Then he intended to take his time, slowly and carefully aiming to kill.

Following the traditional rules of dueling, Dickinson and Jackson each took eight paces across the field and turned his side toward his opponent. As soon as Dickinson had leveled his pistol and fired, a puff of dust rose from the breast of Jackson's coat. To Dickinson's horror, Jackson stood perfectly still, clenching his teeth. Stunned, Dickinson stepped back from his dueling position and cried, "Great God! Have I missed him?"

Little did Dickinson realize that he had failed to consider the politician's thin frame and loose jacket when he had aimed at Jackson's heart. To continue the duel, Jackson's comrades forced Dickinson back to his position. Jackson slowly raised his pistol, carefully aimed, and pulled the trigger. Although the hammer stopped at the half-cock position, Jackson cocked his pistol and fired again. This time, the bullet pierced Dickinson just below the ribs. Dickinson reeled as the bullet seared through his abdomen and lodged into the opposite side of his ribs.

As Dickinson's friends tended to his wounds, Jackson quietly slipped from the field. When an observer noticed that Jackson's shoe was full of blood, Jackson remarked that he had no desire to give Dickinson the satisfaction of knowing that he had even scratched him. Ironically, the bullet fired from Dickinson's pistol remained lodged in Jackson's shoulder for years, eventually leading to his death in 1845.

Dickinson died later in the evening at a local boardinghouse. In the months following the duel, many argued that the rules of dueling prohibited Jackson from pulling the trigger a second time. Others expressed their regret over Dickinson's death, claiming that the duel had been nothing short of murder. Critics continued to discuss the controversial duel throughout Jackson's presidential campaigns of 1824 and 1828, attempting to raise questions about the candidate's character and integrity.

The Mysterious Death of Meriwether Lewis

• 1809 •

As Meriwether Lewis traveled along the Natchez Trace on October 10, 1809, he approached Grinder's Stand, a small inn located about 70 miles from Nashville, Tennessee. But as Lewis arranged overnight lodging at the inn, little did anyone realize that Grinder's Stand would be the final stop of Lewis's life.

Although the Natchez Trace, a pioneer road between Nashville and Natchez, Mississippi, was notorious for robbery and murders, Lewis was accustomed to traveling in dangerous territories. With Captain William Clark, Lewis had led an expedition to the Pacific Ocean between 1804 and 1806. After exploring the vast territory acquired by the United States through the Louisiana Purchase, Lewis and Clark had been hailed as heroes. In fact, President Thomas Jefferson honored Lewis for his efforts by rewarding him with the governorship of the Upper Louisiana Territory.

But the tides turned on Lewis when President Jefferson left office. Jefferson's political opponents refused to pay debts that Lewis had accrued as the first American governor of the Louisiana Territory, leaving the explorer personally liable for the expenses. Determined to resolve the matter, Lewis packed his bags to head for Washington.

Lewis embarked on his journey in late September, accompanied by two servants and Major James Neely, a government agent for the Chickasaw Indians. According to reports from witnesses, Lewis displayed bizarre behavior during the journey, often drinking excessively. While traveling down the Mississippi River, Lewis tried to commit suicide on two occasions, attempting to jump overboard and trying to shoot himself. During a stop at Fort Pickering, located at the present site of Memphis, the fort commander held Lewis on twenty-four-hour suicide watch for more than a week. Moreover, Major Neely later confided to Thomas Jefferson that Lewis "appeared at times deranged in mind" throughout the trip.

On October 10, the morning after crossing the Tennessee River, Neely discovered two of his horses had strayed from their campsite during the night. Promising to meet Lewis at the next inn along the Natchez Trace, Neely stayed behind to look for the stray horses. Lewis continued on his way, riding alone along the rugged trail. Two servants trailed behind him, burdened by heavy trunks.

When Lewis arrived at Grinder's Stand, he informed Mrs. Grinder that Neely and the servants would arrive later. In the absence of her husband, Mrs. Grinder provided the sole source of information about Lewis's arrival and stay at the inn, offering several versions of her story over the years. According to her accounts, Lewis ate little supper, appeared angry, paced his room for several hours, and talked aloud to himself. At three o'clock in the morning, the sound of a gunshot awakened Mrs. Grinder. Then she heard a heavy thud, followed by the words, "Oh, Lord!" and another pistol shot. Several minutes later, Lewis called, "Oh, madam! Give me some water and heal my wounds."

Too frightened to move, Mrs. Grinder crouched for fear in her room. At dawn, she and the servants entered Lewis's room. Alive on the bed, Lewis revealed his bullet wounds to the group and offered money to anyone who would put him out of his misery. A few hours later, he died at the age of thirty-five. He was buried near the site of his death, a short distance from Hohenwald, Tennessee, on land that now belongs to the National Park Service.

With the alleged reports about Lewis's suicide attempts, heavy drinking, and bouts of depression, most believed that distress over his impending financial doom led to a suicidal death. Some, however, contended he was murdered during an attempted robbery. Local residents blamed everyone from bandits to the Grinder family, even speculating that Major Neelly or the men's servants may have murdered Lewis after they arrived at Grinder's Stand.

Even today, a group that includes scholars, forensic scientists, and about 160 of Lewis's descendants continue the quest to solve the mystery of Lewis's death. The group has appealed to the National Park Service to exhume Lewis's body, hoping to determine if he committed suicide or if he was the victim of murder by using such cutting-edge forensic techniques as DNA testing. The National Park Service, however, has denied requests to remove Lewis's remains, leaving the mystery unsolved.

The New Madrid Earthquakes
• 1811-1812 •

A series of intense jolts awakened residents of the western portion of Tennessee shortly after two o'clock on the morning of December 16, 1811, convincing many people that the world was coming to an end. Little did anyone realize that the region was shaking from the first of three major earthquakes that would become known as some of the most violent quakes in the history of North America.

Although most Americans associate earthquakes with the Pacific Coast states, three powerful quakes known as the New Madrid earthquakes shook the region along the Mississippi River in 1811 and 1812. The quakes were named after New Madrid, the closest settlement to the center of the quakes, in the territory of Missouri. If the Richter scale had existed in 1811, scientists believe the quakes would have measured more than 8.0. The quake zone covered more than 1 million square miles, an area two to three times larger than the 1964 Alaska earthquake and ten times larger than the 1906 San Francisco earthquake.

Tremors were felt as far away as Pittsburgh, Pennsylvania, and Norfolk, Virginia, but the greatest impact of the quakes occurred in the Mississippi River region. The December earthquake uplifted large areas of land, created landslides, and flooded sunken areas. Fissures opened and closed beneath the

Mississippi River, generating large waves that capsized many boats and washed some vessels ashore. High banks caved and collapsed into the river, entire islands disappeared, and the mighty Mississippi flowed backward for a brief time.

Although the area was sparsely settled and many residents were illiterate, several witnesses recorded their experiences, including the Scottish naturalist John Bradbury. While sleeping on a boat in the vicinity of Chickasaw Bluffs near the present site of Memphis, Bradbury and his party were awakened by "a most tremendous noise" during the wee hours of December 16. "All nature seemed running into chaos as wild fowl fled, trees snapped and riverbanks tumbled into the water," he later wrote.

Another account by Eliza Bryan of New Madrid reveals the frightening horror of the quake. "The screams of the affrighted inhabitants running to and fro, not knowing where to go, or what to do—the cries of the fowls and beasts of every species—the cracking of trees falling, and the roaring of the Mississippi—the current of which was retrograde for a few minutes, owing as is supposed, to an irruption in its bed—formed a scene truly horrible."

After the December quake, light shocks continued for several weeks. On January 23, 1812, a second earthquake shook the region, producing results similar to the first tremor. One newspaper printed an excerpt of a letter from a Tennessee resident recounting his experiences on the day of the second earthquake:

January 23d, 1812

This morning we were again alarmed by a most tremendous concussion of nature's elements, equal, if not more terrifying than those of the 15th of last month. Its continuation was from 20 to 30 minutes— it shook off the top of one chimney in this town, and

unroofed some small buildings in the neighbour-
hood. It was succeeded by three or four small shocks
in the course of an hour. About 4 o'clock P.M. another
was sensibly felt, but in a much lighter degree.

Following the January quake, "the earth was in continual
agitation, visibly waving as a gentle sea" for several weeks, according to Bryan's account. Then, on the night of February 6,
1812, and the morning of February 7, the most forceful of the
three earthquakes occurred. The third quake destroyed the town
of New Madrid, uplifted large areas of land, and created huge
sunken areas. The quake even cracked walls and knocked down
chimneys in Nashville, according to a report from Andrew Jackson.

One large sunken area filled with water, according to
Bryan's letter: "Lately it has been discovered that a lake was
formed on the opposite side of the Mississippi, in the Indian
country, upwards of one hundred miles in length, and from
one to six miles in width, of the depth of ten to fifty feet."

Bryan correctly reported the phenomena, referring to a
lake in the northwestern portion of Tennessee. Now known as
Reelfoot Lake, the body of water covers eighteen thousand
acres over portions of Lake County and Obion County in Tennessee. Today the lake still contains stumps of trees killed by
the sudden submergence of the ground during the earthquake.

America's First Antislavery Newspaper
• 1819 •

Long before President Abraham Lincoln issued the Emancipation Proclamation in 1863, the ideal of freedom for slaves burned brightly in Tennessee. In 1819, Jonesborough resident Elihu Embree spoke out against slavery by publishing the first newspaper dedicated to the abolitionist cause.

A prominent member of the Religious Society of Friends, Embree and his family strongly supported the Quakers' high standards of social justice for all, including freedom for black slaves in the South. A letter from Embree's father, Thomas, appeared in the *Knoxville Gazette* in 1797, publicly promoting the idea of forming a society dedicated to banning slavery.

When Thomas Embree moved to Ohio around 1806, Elihu Embree remained in Tennessee to take over his family's thriving iron business. At the same time, he continued to promote his father's cause. In 1815, Embree became an active member of the Tennessee Manumission Society, a group that promoted the gradual elimination of slavery and the extension of the Declaration of Independence to all individuals. When members of the group promoted the idea of publishing a newspaper, Embree agreed to serve as editor and to provide financial backing for the venture.

In March 1819, Embree published the first issue of the *Manumission Intelligencer,* America's first antislavery publication, in Jonesborough, Tennessee. Distributed on Tuesdays, the *Manumission Intelligencer* not only promoted the abolitionist cause but also reported on agricultural, cultural, and foreign affairs. Advertisements appeared in the weekly newspaper, including some for the Embree family's iron business. Subscriptions cost three dollars per year, payable in advance.

But Embree soon discovered that he could not devote enough time to the weekly newspaper while he continued to run the iron business. Early in 1820, Embree changed the format to a monthly publication, known as *The Emancipator,* devoted solely to abolitionist causes. Published in a journal-style, magazine format, the premiere issue of *The Emancipator* appeared on April 30, 1820. Although the first issue attracted only six paid subscribers at a cost of one dollar per year, circulation increased rapidly. By June, Embree was printing more than 2,500 copies to meet the demand.

Despite his personal commitment to the abolitionist cause, Embree became a slave owner as a result of his second marriage to Elizabeth Worley Carriger in 1808. About a year after the marriage, Embree sold the family of slaves to two buyers. He bought back the slaves in 1812, and most historians believe that Embree repurchased the slaves in order to release them from slavery. However, Embree owned one female slave and her five children at the time of his death. His last will and testament named each of his remaining slaves and provided that they should be "legally emancipated as soon as they can." Still, he admitted in one issue of *The Emancipator* that he was "not very scrupulous in adhering to what I believed to be right, as respected much of my moral conduct."

But not even the financial burden of publishing *The Emancipator* could prevent Embree from voicing his support for the abolitionist movement. In one issue of the publication, he noted:

Altho' the editor is as far from being a man of leisure as any of his acquaintances . . . he has spent several thousand dollars already in some small degree abolishing slavery . . . hoping . . . in small degree [it will] hasten an even balance of equal rights to the now neglected sons of Africa.

The hope of freedom for slaves apparently inspired Embree to continue his quest. In another issue of *The Emancipator,* he wrote:

Twenty years ago the cause of abolition was so unpopular in Tennessee, that it was at the [risk] of a man's life that he interfered or assisted in establishing the liberty of a person of color that was held in slavery. . . . But by little & little, times are much changed here, until societies of respectable citizens have arisen to plead the cause of abolition.

After publishing seven issues of *The Emancipator,* Embree died of unknown causes in December 1820, at the age of thirty-eight. Returning to Tennessee for a short time, Thomas Embree tried to continue his son's mission by recruiting a fellow Quaker, Benjamin Lundy, to take over the publication. But instead of resuming *The Emancipator* in Jonesborough, Lundy moved to Greeneville to publish his own abolitionist newspaper, *The Genius of Universal Emancipation.* Lundy later moved the newspaper to Baltimore.

After Elihu Embree's death, his son-in-law, Thomas Jefferson Wilson, recognized the importance of Embree's publications and preserved the issues for the future by binding them into book form in 1833. More than a century later, the Tennessee State Legislature honored the memory of Elihu Embree for his work on behalf of the "universal and equal liberty of all men," calling for the reissue of the *Manumission Intelligencer* and *The Emancipator* in book form.

The Invention of the Cherokee Alphabet

• 1821 •

He was born with a congenital deformity, but physical handicaps did not prevent him from creating both an alphabet and a written language. Known as Sequoyah, this Cherokee from the village of Tuskegee, in present-day Tennessee, developed a writing system for his people.

Born about 1776 near the present town of Vonore on the Little Tennessee River, Sequoyah was the son of Nathaniel Gist, a white fur trader, and Wut-teh, the daughter of a Cherokee chief. Historians believe Sequoyah was born with a club foot. Although his English name was George, the young boy was known as Sequoyah, a Cherokee name meaning "pig's foot."

From an early age, Sequoyah was fascinated by the white settlers' marks on paper. A skilled silversmith who eventually established a trading post, Sequoyah never learned the English alphabet. But as white silversmiths began to sign their silver pieces, customers requested Sequoyah's signature on his silver products, as well. Unable to write, Sequoyah turned to a white neighbor for help. After learning how to spell his name in English, Sequoyah began to work on creating a writing system for the Cherokee people in 1809.

The War of 1812 deepened Sequoyah's awareness of the need for a Cherokee writing system. Despite his handicap, Sequoyah served in the Cherokee Regiment, fighting against

British troops and the Creek Indians under the leadership of General Andrew Jackson. Unlike white soldiers, Sequoyah and most other Cherokee could not read military orders or write letters to their families at home. After he returned home from the war, Sequoyah focused his efforts on developing a written Cherokee language.

Sequoyah determined the Cherokee language was comprised of sounds and combinations of vowels and consonants. Using a phonetic system, Sequoyah developed eighty-five symbols that represented all of the sounds that formed the Cherokee language. After his young daughter, Anyoka, easily learned the symbols, Sequoyah began to teach his new syllabary to others.

In 1821, Sequoyah introduced the writing system to a gathering of tribal leaders. Astonished by Sequoyah's convincing demonstration, the National Council of the Cherokees approved the syllabary as the Cherokee's official, national language system. Within a few months, thousands of Cherokee men, women, and children had learned to read and write by using Sequoyah's symbols. By 1825, much of the Bible and numerous hymns had been translated into Cherokee.

Sequoyah's writing system soon paved the way for the establishment of the first Indian newspaper in the United States. After purchasing a printing press, the National Council launched the *Cherokee Phoenix* on February 21, 1828, the nation's first bilingual newspaper. The council also produced pamphlets, educational materials, and legal documents for the Cherokee, using Sequoyah's writing system. In honor of his accomplishments, Sequoyah received a medal from the Cherokee Nation and an award of five hundred dollars from the United States Congress.

In 1829, Sequoyah moved to the Oklahoma Territory to help teach the writing system to other tribes. He continued to serve the Cherokee people as a statesman and diplomat until his death in 1843 in northern Mexico. Today, he is credited as the only person in history to create both an alphabet and a written language.

The Cherokee Removal

· 1838 ·

In the late 1830s, thousands of Cherokees were forced to leave their native homeland in the southeastern region of the United States for new lands west of the Mississippi River. For many Cherokee, this tragic journey, known as the Trail of Tears, originated at Ross's Landing on the Tennessee River.

Shortly after the end of the Creek War, John Ross established Ross's Landing as a trading post. By the mid-1830s, Ross's Landing had become a popular stop for traders along the Tennessee River. Three stores, a tavern, and a small warehouse operated from the site, as well as a ferry service that provided transportation across the river. Cherokee from the surrounding area frequently traded with the owner of Ross's Landing, who was one-eighth Cherokee.

The signing of the New Echota Treaty in 1835 by a small group of Cherokees mandated the removal of all the Cherokees from the region. By the summer of 1836, five companies of volunteer soldiers had arrived at Ross's Landing to prepare for the peaceable removal of the Cherokee. After clearing some land, the soldiers used fallen timber to build a crude fort with log cabins that could provide shelter for about one hundred people. Then the soldiers searched the surrounding area for Cherokee and brought them to the fort at Ross's Landing.

By March 1837, several hundred Indians had been imprisoned within the stockade. To prepare for moving the Cherokee from the fort, a physician arrived to examine them. Surprisingly, he discovered a healthy group, finding only one case of a common cold. But as a flotilla of flatboats arrived at the landing to pick up a large group of Cherokees, the physician discovered that some of the Indians had broken into several whiskey barrels on the shore. By departure time, the men had become highly intoxicated and "very rude and noisy." Accompanied by a detachment of soldiers, the men were forced to board the flatboats with nearly two hundred other Cherokees. The group departed Ross's Landing on March 3, 1837.

Throughout the remainder of the year, the Cherokee firmly resisted the soldiers' attempts to remove them from their native lands. In May 1838, the federal government charged General Winfield Scott with the responsibility of removing the Cherokee from the region by the end of the year. Additional soldiers were dispatched to Ross's Landing with new instructions to capture resistant Cherokee and to bring them to the stockade. One of the soldiers was an army lieutenant named Braxton Bragg, who later served in the Civil War as a Confederate general.

Following orders, the soldiers seized hundreds of Cherokees from the area. Stripped of their possessions and robbed of their homes, captured Cherokee and their animals were herded into the stockades at Ross's Landing. As one correspondent later wrote:

The scenes of distress exhibited at Ross's Landing defy all description. On the arrival there of the Indians, the horses brought by some of them were demanded by the commissioners of Indian property, to be given up for the purpose of being sold. The owners refused to give them up—men, women, children and horses were driven promiscuously into one large pen, and the horses taken out by force, and [auctioned] off to the highest bidder, and sold for almost nothing.

To prepare for moving the Cherokee from the area, military authorities solicited bids from farmers in the region. Many local farmers supplied the government with beef, salt pork, bacon, corn, cornmeal, flour, and salt. The food was then divided and rationed into small portions for each Cherokee.

On June 6, 1838, the first party of Indians departed Ross's Landing. Accompanied by soldier guards, about eight hundred Cherokees from nearby Georgia were packed into six flatboats and a 100-ton steamship. One of the flatboats contained a double-decked cabin. Three of the flatboats, each 20 feet wide and 130 feet in length, were lashed together on either side of the steamer. In the rush and excitement of pushing the Cherokee onto the boats, authorities failed to conduct an official head count of the departing Indians.

One week later, on June 13, a second party of 875 captive Cherokees were placed on six flatboats at Ross's Landing and transferred to Brown's Ferry, located a few miles away, to wait for the arrival of another group of Indians. During the two-day stay at Brown's Ferry, most of the Indians refused to accept gifts of clothing from the government and declined to reveal their names to the guards. After the arrival of the second group, the entire party continued on their westward journey.

A third party of nearly eleven hundred Cherokees departed Ross's Landing on June 17. Ordered to march overland, the group headed for Waterloo, Alabama. The plan was that after arriving at Waterloo, the group would board boats to continue their journey by water. But after three days of marching in unbearably hot weather, the Indians pleaded with the emigration superintendent to postpone the remainder of the journey until cooler weather arrived. Although the Cherokee offered to return to Ross's Landing or to another camp and remain imprisoned until the end of the summer season, their requests were denied. The march continued.

Serving as the principal chief of the Cherokee Nation, John Ross focused his full attention on the plight of the Cherokee people. Convinced that the Indians could not endure the harsh conditions of a long journey during the sweltering summer months, Ross persuaded General Scott to postpone the remainder of the Cherokee removal until fall. Moreover, Ross received permission to take charge of the final removal efforts, agreeing that the Indians would be on their way by October 20.

Some 2,500 Cherokees remained imprisoned at Ross's Landing throughout the summer of 1838. In October, John Ross, his family, and the remaining Cherokees departed for their new homeland in the West. Ross's wife, Quatie, died during the journey, along with hundreds of other Cherokees. In later years, a major settlement blossomed around the site of the stockade at Ross's Landing, developing into a city that is now known as Chattanooga.

The Volunteers of Tennessee

· 1846 ·

When President James Knox Polk issued a call for volunteers to fight in the Mexican War in 1846, Americans flocked to recruiting centers across the nation. No state produced more volunteers than the president's home state. Volunteers from · Tennessee responded in overwhelming numbers, earning a permanent place in history for their patriotic spirit.

The drums of war sounded for Americans soon after the admission of Texas into the Union in 1845. Determined to reclaim the state as part of Mexico, Mexican soldiers crossed the border and attacked Texas settlers in April 1846. Within the next month, the U.S. Congress had declared war on Mexico for "invading United States territory."

The American army was too small to fight effectively against the Mexican forces. At the outbreak of the conflict, fewer than seven thousand soldiers were serving in the U.S. Army. To increase the number of active American troops, Congress authorized the enlistment of fifty thousand volunteers to serve for a period of one year. Quotas were assigned to states located near Texas, including most of the southern states. Tennessee's quota was 2,800 volunteers.

Waves of enthusiasm for the military swept through Tennessee, flooding recruiting stations with volunteers. By the time Tennessee received the news about its quota from the nation's capital, nearly thirty thousand Tennesseans had volunteered to serve—over ten times the state's quota. In the end, a state lottery determined which volunteers would go to war. Several zealous Tennesseans actually paid for the chance to serve their country, convincing lucky lottery winners to accept payments in exchange for their slots.

A total of about seventy-five thousand Americans served as volunteers in the Mexican War, eliminating the need for a draft. Fighting ended when troops led by General Winfield Scott defeated the Mexican army and captured Mexico City in September 1847. Although American forces suffered almost thirteen thousand deaths during the war, only seventeen hundred soldiers died in combat or from battle injuries. Most deaths occurred from diseases or illnesses such as dysentery and malaria, which often resulted from the poor sanitary conditions in camps.

Because recruiting stations had not been established for every Tennessee county and some recruiters signed up men from various counties, a complete roster of Tennessee volunteers in the Mexican War was never compiled. But military service remained high on the list of priorities of Tennessee residents throughout the nineteenth century. During the Civil War, more men from Tennessee served in the Confederate Army than any other southern state, totaling around one hundred thousand soldiers. Moreover, Tennessee furnished the Union with fifty thousand soldiers, more than nine northern states.

It was the patriotic zeal and overwhelming number of volunteers from Tennessee during the Mexican War, however, that etched a permanent spot in history. In honor of thousands of Tennesseans who were willing to serve their country during a time of war, Tennessee became known as the "Volunteer State," a nickname that continues to serve as a reminder of Tennessee's spirit of patriotism during the Mexican War.

The Battle of Shiloh
• 1862 •

At the first light of dawn on April 6, 1862, the day seemed full of promise and hope to the forty-two thousand Union soldiers camped along the west bank of the Tennessee River. "It was a most beautiful morning," a Union private from Indiana later recalled. "It really seemed like Sunday in the country at home. The boys were scattered around . . . polishing and brightening their muskets and brushing up and cleaning their shoes, jackets, [and] trousers." Within a short time, however, everything changed for the private and his comrades. Confederate troops stormed into the peaceful setting, taking the Union troops by surprise and launching one of the bloodiest battles of the Civil War.

For nearly a month, Union troops under the command of General Ulysses S. Grant had been waiting beside the river for the arrival of General Don Carlos Buell and the Army of the Ohio. Together, the forces intended to advance into Mississippi. But Confederate General Albert Sidney Johnston had other plans in store for Grant's men. After suffering defeat at Fort Henry and Fort Donelson, Johnston had withdrawn from Tennessee and headed for Corinth, Mississippi, located some 20 miles south of Pittsburg Landing. In early April 1862, Johnston decided to move his troops north and attack Grant before Buell's reinforcements arrived on the scene.

At about nine-thirty in the morning, the Confederates charged into the Union camp and opened fire. Caught by surprise, Union troops struggled to defend themselves as nearly forty thousand Confederates swept through the area. By mid-morning, victory seemed within reach for Johnston and his men.

But the Union troops held their ground, putting up a savage fight on a hill near a little Methodist church known as Shiloh. Although more than four hundred Confederate soldiers stormed up the hill to attack the Union troops, only one hundred survived the ascent. More brutal fighting took place in a peach orchard as Union forces grappled against fierce Confederate attacks. Amid the heavy casualties, not even General Johnston could escape the wrath of enemy fire. A Union bullet sliced into Johnston's leg as he led the last charge into the orchard. Although he was initially too involved in the fighting to realize that he'd been hit, Johnston soon discovered his boot was filled with blood. Before a doctor could be summoned, the general bled to death on the battlefield from a severed artery.

Confederates surrounded the remaining Union soldiers in a dense oak thicket known as the "Hornet's Nest." Although Grant's men withstood nearly six hours of Confederate assaults, they could not resist the forceful power of the enemy's many guns. By late afternoon, the Union division at the Hornet's Nest had surrendered to the Confederates.

Upon Johnston's death, Confederate command at Shiloh passed to General Pierre G. T. Beauregard. Because the Confederates had gained 2 miles of Union ground throughout the day, Beauregard was satisfied that victory was at hand. That evening, he sent a wire to Confederate President Jefferson Davis, stating that he had won "a complete victory." Little did he realize that twenty-five thousand fresh Union troops had just arrived by steamboat.

Throughout the night, the fighting continued. Union gunboats fired shells into the Confederate camps, masking the sounds of General Buell's reinforcements as they assumed their positions. By dawn the next day, the weary Confederates realized that they were outnumbered. Suffering heavy losses, the Confederates fell back, counterattacked, then fell back again. In late afternoon, Beauregard withdrew his men from the field and retreated to Corinth.

All in all, one hundred thousand men fought at Shiloh. For many soldiers on both sides, Shiloh was their first taste of war. Eight out of ten soldiers involved in the fighting had never experienced combat. Some were unaccustomed to following orders, many were unfamiliar with battle commands, and nearly one in four was a casualty. By the time the fighting ended at Shiloh on April 7, 1862, the conflict had become the bloodiest battle of the Civil War. Over twenty thousand soldiers were killed, wounded, captured, or declared missing. Three thousand four hundred seventy-seven men died—more than the combined number of all Americans who died in battle during the Revolutionary War, the War of 1812, and the Mexican War.

At the onset of the Civil War, many people believed that the conflict would not be a lengthy one. But the high casualties and fierce fighting at the Battle of Shiloh changed America's expectations about the war. As Grant recalled in later years, "Up to the battle of Shiloh, I, as well as thousands of other citizens, believed that the rebellion against the Government would collapse suddenly and soon if a decisive victory could be gained over any of its armies . . . but [afterward] I gave up all idea of saving the Union except by complete conquest."

The Battle of Shiloh derived its name from the small Shiloh Methodist church, the site of some of the fiercest fighting of the battle. Ironically, *Shiloh* is a Hebrew word meaning "place of peace." Since 1894, Shiloh National Military Park has preserved the 4,000-acre battlefield in Hardin County, Tennessee, establishing a lasting tribute to the men who fought and died in one of the bloodiest battles of the Civil War.

The Making of a Confederate Hero

• 1863 •

Union soldiers stood in silence, surrounding the scaffold on a hillside that overlooked the town of Pulaski, Tennessee. A hangman's noose waited for Private Sam Davis, a Tennessee soldier who had been tried, convicted, and sentenced to hang for his role as a Confederate spy. As Davis slowly approached the gallows on that fair November morning in 1863, Union troops were astonished by the young soldier's heroic stand in the face of death.

A Confederate soldier from Smyrna, Tennessee, Davis had volunteered for the First Tennessee Infantry in 1861. As a private, he received several commendations for valor during the Battle of Shiloh and the First Valley Campaign of 1862 in the Shenandoah Valley. He also participated in battles at Perryville, Murfreesboro (Stones River), and Shelbyville. By July 1862, Davis was selected to serve as a member of a special cavalry company that was charged with the mission of providing General Braxton Bragg with detailed information on Union troop and supply movements. The elite company of soldiers reported directly to Dr. H. B. Shaw, who assumed the alias of "Captain Coleman" for the undercover operations. Davis and his comrades were known as "Coleman's Scouts."

In the fall of 1863, Davis gathered information on Union fortifications and movements within the city of Nashville. Captain Shaw ordered Davis to deliver the information to General Bragg in Chattanooga. On the morning of November 20, Davis set off on his mission wearing a faded Union overcoat over his Confederate uniform and hiding the valuable documents in his saddle and the soles of his boots.

As he traveled down a rural road about 15 miles south of Pulaski, he encountered two soldiers dressed in Confederate uniforms who claimed they were conscripting for the Confederacy. Davis insisted that he was already a Confederate soldier, promptly revealing his pass and pointing out that he was wearing a Confederate uniform beneath his overcoat.

Unbeknown to Davis, the two men in Confederate uniforms were actually Union soldiers. The soldiers promptly arrested Davis and led him to their commanding officer, General Grenville Dodge, in Pulaski. While conducting a search of Davis's personal effects, the Union soldiers discovered detailed documents that revealed information on Nashville's fortifications and Union positions and movements. They also discovered a letter from Captain Coleman to General Bragg that recorded the activities of Coleman's Scouts.

Union officers interrogated Davis for several days, demanding the source of his information and the identity of Captain Coleman. "I tried to impress upon him the danger he was in and that I knew he was only a messenger, and held out to him the hope of lenient treatment if he would answer truthfully, as far as he could, my questions," General Dodge later recalled.

Throughout the interrogation, Davis revealed nothing to his captors. No one could ignore his courage and strong sense of personal honor. Although many Union officers encouraged Davis to talk so his life would be spared, the young man remained silent. Unable to get answers, General Dodge warned Davis that he would be convicted as a spy and sentenced to hang if he refused to cooperate. Dodge promised Davis his freedom and a horse if Davis revealed the information. To Dodge's amazement, Davis "very quietly and firmly refused to do it."

On November 25, General Dodge convened a court-martial, which quickly resulted in a verdict of guilty and a sentence of death by hanging. On the day before his execution, Davis penned his last letter to his parents, Charles Louise and Jane Simmons Davis, of Rutherford County, Tennessee:

Pulaski, Giles County, Tenn., Nov. 26, 1863

Dear Mother:

Oh, how painful it is to write you! I have got to die tomorrow morning—to be hanged by the Federals. Mother, do not grieve for me. I must bid you good-by forevermore. Mother, I do not fear to die. Give my love to all.

Your son, Samuel Davis

Mother, tell the children all to be good. I wish I could see you all once more, but I never will any more.

Mother and Father, do not forget me. Think of me when I am dead, but do not grieve for me. It will not do any good. Father, you can send after my remains if you want to do so. They will be at Pulaski, Tenn. I will leave some things, too, with the hotel keeper for you. Pulaski is in Giles county, Tenn., south of Columbia. S.D.

On the morning of November 27, 1863, Union guards transported Davis from the Giles County jail to a hillside in East Pulaski for the execution. Davis rode in a wagon seated upon his own coffin. As Davis climbed the steps to the gallows, the provost marshal reminded the young man that it was not too late to reveal the source of his information. Would he not save himself and identify Coleman?

Davis's answer was full of resolve, echoing the sentiments of patriot Nathan Hale during the American Revolution: "Do you suppose that I would betray a friend? No, sir! I would die a thousand times first!" After a prayer with the chaplain, he turned to the provost marshal and announced, "I am ready."

Less than two months after his twenty-first birthday, Private Sam Davis was hanged as a Confederate spy. But the memory of Davis' sacrifice lingered long after the hangman's noose tightened around his neck. Years later, a Union private recalled, "I could not forget, nor have I to this day forgotten, that boy hero," admitting that witnessing "such a pathetic and heroic scene" had sent "tears streaming down [his] face."

Pauline Cushman's Escape

· 1863 ·

In 1863, she was convicted and sentenced to hang for her role as a Union spy. But actress Pauline Cushman cleverly used her dramatic skills to escape from the hangman's noose in Shelbyville, Tennessee.

Born in 1835, Cushman was a New Orleans native who moved to Michigan at an early age. Her real name was Harriet Wood, but she assumed the name of Pauline Cushman to pursue a theatrical career. By age seventeen, she was appearing in New York theaters. Although she was married for a brief time, her husband died during the early years of the Civil War.

Touring with a theatrical company, the actress performed onstage throughout the nation during the war. Cushman's attractive appearance pleased audiences and snared the attention of the press. One newspaper described her features as "perfect—so perfect that the sculptor's imagination would fail to add a single point, or banish a single blemish."

During one of Cushman's 1863 appearances at Wood's Theatre in Louisville, Kentucky, two paroled Confederate officers presented the actress with an intriguing proposal. Would she toast Confederate President Jefferson Davis and the Confederacy during her performance—for the sum of three hundred dollars? Because Kentucky was a Union state, Cushman quickly reported the bribe to Union officers. Hoping that many members of the audience would reveal their Southern sympathies by cheering the toast, the officers encouraged Cushman to accept the challenge.

Cushman resumed her performance, stepping to the front of the stage. Lifting a champagne glass, she shouted, "Here's to Jefferson Davis and the Southern Confederacy. May the South always maintain her honor and her rights!"

Confederate sympathizers cheered, while Union supporters booed. Union officials sitting in the audience quickly pretended to arrest the actress in a mock attempt to warn other Confederate sympathizers of their fate if they continued to support the Southern cause. Moreover, the theatrical company promptly fired Cushman for her outburst.

Impressed with Cushman's acting skills, the chief of police with the Army of the Cumberland quickly recruited the actress to serve in the Union's secret service. Cushman signed an oath of service to the Army of the Cumberland on May 26, 1863. She soon became an expert in counterespionage, or spying on enemy spies. She identified several Southern spies and learned many of their secret methods for sending messages. She also obtained information on the movement of Confederate supplies and the operation of guerrilla troops.

In the spring of 1863, Union officials in Nashville asked Cushman to obtain information about Confederate troops under the command of General Braxton Bragg. Pretending to search for her lost brother, Cushman followed Bragg's troops through Kentucky and Tennessee. But the deceptive mission ended near Nashville when Confederate soldiers discovered important papers in her possession. According to one newspaper account, "the fair and brave Pauline was taken in the dead of night by rebel scouts while she was resting at the house of . . . a farmer residing near the Hardin turnpike road."

Cushman was escorted to the headquarters of Confederate General Nathan Bedford Forrest. Although Cushman maintained that she was a loyal Confederate, Forrest ordered an investigation of her activities. She was then transported to General Bragg's headquarters in Shelbyville, Tennessee. As Bragg grilled the actress about her identity, Cushman asked, "But if I am found guilty, what will you do with me?"

The general replied, "You will surely be hanged."

As Bragg had predicted, Cushman was found guilty of spying for the Union and sentenced to die by hanging. But "Miss Pauline was taken exceedingly ill" shortly after her conviction, and Confederate officials postponed the execution until she could recover from her illness. Most believe, however, that Cushman called upon her dramatic skills and feigned serious illness to delay the fatal punishment.

After three months of captivity in Shelbyville, Cushman received an unexpected reprieve. When Union forces attacked the Tennessee town, the Confederate soldiers fled without her. Left behind by the Confederate troops, Cushman not only escaped the hangman's noose but also gained her freedom.

With her identity revealed, Cushman's career as a spy ended. Treated as a hero by the Union forces, she received an honorary major's commission from President Abraham Lincoln. She returned to the stage, presenting a monologue about her adventures as a spy while wearing her major's uniform. Furthermore, author Ferdinand Sarmiento captured Cushman's adventures on paper, using her notes to write the book *The Life of Pauline Cushman.*

During her later years, Pauline Cushman moved to San Francisco and lived a meager life. She died from an overdose of opium in 1893. The Grand Army of the Republic (GAR), an organization of Civil War veterans, gave her a full military funeral, including an honor guard and a rifle salute. She was buried in the GAR cemetery in San Francisco.

The *Sultana* Disaster
• 1865 •

Nothing seemed unusual about the *Sultana*'s departure from New Orleans in the spring of 1865. Weighing nearly seventeen hundred tons, the sturdy steamship appeared to be making a normal run as she chugged her way up the mighty Mississippi. But the *Sultana*'s routine voyage took a tragic turn near Memphis, Tennessee, resulting in the worst maritime disaster in American history.

Built in 1863, the *Sultana* routinely carried passengers and cargo between New Orleans and major cities along the Mississippi River. On April 21, 1865, the *Sultana* departed New Orleans for another routine voyage to Cairo, Illinois, carrying eighty-five crew members, around one hundred cabin passengers, and an assortment of cargo and livestock.

Despite raging, flood-level waters, the *Sultana* stayed on course for the next three days. By the time the ship made a scheduled stop at Vicksburg, Mississippi, however, a leak had developed in one of the steamer's boilers. The ship's captain, J. C. Mason, decided to lay over in Vicksburg until the boiler could be repaired. While the repair crew scurried to patch the leaking boiler, the *Sultana* prepared to welcome aboard new passengers. With a capacity of 375, the steamer had room for several more passengers on this particular river voyage.

But far more than a few passengers were waiting to board the *Sultana* at the Vicksburg wharf. In fact, about two thousand

Union soldiers eagerly waited to catch a ride on the steamer. Two weeks earlier, the war had essentially ended with Confederate General Robert E. Lee's surrender to Union General Ulysses S. Grant at Appomattox Courthouse in Virginia. Former prisoners of war, the soldiers had just been released from the horrors of such Confederate prisons as Andersonville and Cahaba. Now that the war was over, the men were eager to return to their families and homes in the North.

Because shipping companies received payment from the federal government for every soldier they transported along the Mississippi River, the *Sultana* welcomed the arrival of the soldiers. Leaping at the chance to go home, men crowded into the vessel before military authorities could prepare muster rolls. Although lacking an official count, authorities estimated that between eighteen hundred and two thousand soldiers jammed onto the *Sultana,* along with the cabin passengers and crew members. In total, more than two thousand people were packed onto a steamship designed for fewer than four hundred passengers.

Thirty-three hours after docking at Vicksburg, the *Sultana* cast off from the wharf and headed upstream. Although the steamship strained beneath the weight of the heavy load, the *Sultana* made several scheduled stops over the next two days. On the evening of April 26, the vessel arrived at Memphis. The repair crew tended to another boiler leak, and several passengers disembarked during the brief stop. By midnight, the *Sultana* was on its way again. Fighting against the powerful currents, the steamer slowly chugged through the high waters. Over the course of the next two hours, the ship traveled only a few miles upstream.

Then disaster struck the *Sultana.* Just as the ship rounded a bend in the river, the boilers exploded, ripping apart the steamship. The explosion instantly killed hundreds of soldiers. Hundreds more were blown into the river from the force of the impact. Hot coals from the furnace blasted through the air, creating balls of fire that quickly spread through the wreckage. Many of the remaining passengers onboard jumped into the water to avoid the spreading flames. Others clung to the derelict ship for dear life, including one survivor who later recalled the horrid scene: "On looking down and out into the river, I would see men jumping from all parts of the boat in the water until it seemed black with men, their heads bobbing up and down like corks, and then disappearing beneath the turbulent waters, never to appear again."

Another survivor remembered his struggle to survive in the water: "When I got about three hundred yards away from the boat, clinging to a heavy plank, the whole heavens seemed to be lighted up by the conflagration. The water seemed to be one solid mass of human beings struggling with the waves."

Helplessly drifting downstream, the *Sultana* began to sink. One portion of the deck collapsed, and the huge twin smokestacks tottered and crashed into the water. The final blow came as the boat struck a small island. Just as the remaining passengers jumped ashore, the remains of the *Sultana* disappeared beneath the muddy waters of the Mississippi.

The sights and sounds of the fiery explosion could be seen and heard for miles along the Mississippi. Numerous riverboats from Memphis rushed to the scene, finding dozens of survivors clinging to logs, planks, and other debris in the river. Unfortunately, little could be done to help many of the victims. As prisoners of war, many passengers had suffered from starvation in prison camps, and most lacked the physical strength to stay afloat. Although rescue craft pulled around 550 men from the water and transported them to Memphis hospitals, about 250 of the survivors later died from burns or injuries. Barges picked up dead bodies for several days after the disaster.

Because a complete list of passengers was never compiled, the precise number of casualties could not be determined. According to some estimates, the *Sultana* explosion resulted in fifteen hundred to nineteen hundred deaths—the worst maritime tragedy in U.S. history.

Unlike the *Titanic* disaster, the *Sultana* tragedy received only moderate attention from the press. During the month of April 1865, Lee's surrender and Lincoln's assassination overshadowed news of the *Sultana*. Even today, few history books mention the tragedy. Although the cities of Knoxville and Memphis erected memorials in honor of the *Sultana,* no federal marker exists to commemorate the incident. Today, what remains of the *Sultana* rests beneath the Mississippi River, buried in the mud at the site of the sinking.

America's First Registered Distillery

• 1866 •

Jasper Newton "Jack" Daniel was simply complying with federal law when he registered his new distillery operations with the government in 1866. Little did he realize that his registration papers would make the Jack Daniel Distillery, Lynchburg, Tennessee, the oldest registered distillery in the country.

Although the federal government started regulating spirits during the Civil War, new regulations for distillers took effect after the war was over. The law not only required every distiller to register with the government, but also imposed a two-dollar tax on every proof gallon of whiskey purchased. Before the new law, distillery operations like Jack Daniel's had not been subject to taxes or government controls. Almost every home kept a jug of whiskey for little celebrations or toddies, and everybody kept some for medicinal purposes.

Even though Daniel was merely twenty years old when he proudly registered his new distillery, the ambitious young man had been making whiskey for more than half his life. As a young boy in Lincoln County, Daniel had learned the art of whiskey-making from a neighbor who used a special process that mellowed the whiskey known as the "Lincoln County Way." The technique used a naturally fermented sour mash whiskey with no chemicals or other additives filtered through 9 to 10 feet of sugar maple charcoal. The area's limestone springs provided another important ingredient in making whiskey. The naturally cold, iron-free water that fed Lincoln County's pools, streams, and creeks cooled the stills during the whiskey-making process.

By the time he was ten years old, Daniel had earned enough money from working at his neighbor's still to buy a team of mules and a wagon. Loading his wagon with whiskey kegs and barrels, he drove to country stores in the area and sold the whiskey. He used his profits to purchase the neighbor's still, establishing his own business at age thirteen.

Though physically small—standing 5 feet, 5 inches and weighing 120 pounds—Daniel had big dreams of expanding his business. He found the perfect spot for building a new distillery at Cave Spring Hollow, an area that flowed with pure spring water from a nearby limestone cave. Situated near the little town of Lynchburg, the site offered easy access to railroad transportation in the larger town of Tullahoma, 15 miles away. By the end of the Civil War, Daniel had relocated the distillery to Cave Spring Hollow.

After the war, many distilleries began to use easier and simpler methods of making whiskey. But Jack Daniel continued to distill whiskey in the time-consuming Lincoln County Way, determined to produce the finest whiskey in the country. To distinguish his products from other spirits on the market, Daniel sold his whiskey in a distinctive square bottle and emphasized the quality of his products, particularly "Jack Daniel's Old Time Sour Mash" and "Old No. 7." In 1896, the *Nashville American* reported:

> The sale of Jack Daniel's pure old sour mash whiskey is affected only by its quality. The goods are in demand. He has no travelling salesmen and does not need any. His whiskey commends itself. It finds ready purchasers wherever it becomes ready for the market. His widely known "No. 7" has attained more

popularity than any other brand of whiskey that has been on the market in many years.

In 1904, Daniel introduced his Tennessee whiskey to the world at the Louisiana Purchase Exposition, more commonly known as the St. Louis World's Fair. A panel of judges awarded a gold medal to Daniel's whiskey, proclaiming it to be "the world's best whiskey." In the following years, Daniel continued to enter his whiskey in global competitions, eventually earning six more international gold medals.

Soon after the St. Louis World's Fair, Daniel suffered an injury that would eventually take his life. Frustrated while trying to unlock his safe, Daniel gave the door a swift kick. The force of the impact cracked his big toe, which later became infected. In light of his declining health, Daniel signed over the business in 1907 to his two nephews, Lem Motlow and Richard Daniel. Daniel hoped the two men would not only oversee the daily operations of the distillery but also help the business survive in the face of Prohibition. Out of one hundred distilleries in Tennessee at the start of the twentieth century, only the Jack Daniel Distillery remained in operation by 1910.

Six years after his encounter with the stubborn safe, Daniel died from complications of his injury, passing away on October 9, 1911, at age sixty-five. An editorial in the *Memphis Herald* stated:

> When the historian of the future comes to write of Tennessee, and reaches Lincoln County, he will probably preface his account with: "It was in that portion of Lincoln which was later to form Moore County that the famous old-time distillery of Jack Daniel was located." The historian will do this because the excellence of the product of that old-time distillery has done more to give fame to Lincoln County than any other factor or set of factors.

After Jack Daniel's death, Motlow soon bought out his cousin and continued to run the Tennessee distillery. When state prohibition laws temporarily closed down the business, Motlow shifted the distillery's operations to Missouri, a state that had not yet become "dry." He later lobbied for the repeal of Tennessee's dry laws, encouraging the state's general assembly to approve the manufacturing of liquor in Tennessee and to sell the liquor outside the state. As a result of his efforts, the Tennessee General Assembly passed the bill in 1937.

Today the Jack Daniel Distillery continues to craft its old-time sipping whiskey in Lynchburg, Tennessee, which is now located in Moore County. A National Historic Site, the oldest registered distillery in the country remains true to its founder's motto: "Each day we make it, we will make it the best we can."

Pulaski's Secret Society

• 1866 •

It was formed as a social fraternity in Pulaski, Tennessee, during the Reconstruction era. Socializing, however, was not the primary purpose of the Ku Klux Klan. To promote an agenda of white supremacy, the organization used violent, aggressive tactics to terrorize members of minority groups throughout the South after the Civil War.

Six former officers of the Confederate Army founded the Ku Klux Klan at Pulaski in 1866. The group derived its name from a Greek word for "circle" or "band" and the English word *clan*. Though originally disguised as a social fraternity, the true purpose of the Ku Klux Klan was to promote superiority of whites and to ensure "voluntary separation" of the races. Secrecy and disguises dominated the activities of the Ku Klux Klan, which was also called the KKK, Klan, and "Invisible Empire."

Nathan Bedford Forrest, a former Confederate general, probably served as the Klan's first leader under the titles of Grand Wizard and Imperial Wizard. Born on July 13, 1821, in Bedford County, Tennessee, Forrest became a wealthy Mississippi cotton planter and slave trader before the Civil War. At the age of forty, he enlisted as a private in the Confederate Army. By the time the war had ended, Forrest had achieved the rank of lieutenant general. No other private in the Confederate or Union armies climbed the ranks as high as Forrest.

On the battlefield, Forrest gained a reputation as the most feared cavalry commander of the Civil War. Twenty-nine horses were shot out from under him, and he was wounded four times in battle. Though hot-tempered and impatient, Forrest was a gifted soldier who won praise from his enemies for his military accomplishments. But despite his military prowess, Forrest was often perceived as a racist. He was responsible for the massacre of blacks at Fort Pillow in 1864.

After the war, Forrest returned to Mississippi to restore his plantation. Learning of the movement to form the KKK, Forrest traveled to Nashville to find out more about the group from an old friend, Captain John Morton, who had served as Forrest's chief of artillery during the war. In May 1866, Morton swore Forrest into the Klan.

Following a brief period of playing practical jokes and pretending to be ghosts, the Klan evolved into a group dedicated to keeping blacks "in their place." Klansmen terrorized blacks to prevent them from exercising the emancipation rights they had recently gained. Secrecy and disguises intrigued KKK members, who concealed their identities by posing as ghosts of dead Confederate soldiers, donning white hoods and cloaks, draping sheets over their horses, and launching attacks on blacks during the night. Disguised Klansmen frequently assembled in a circle at outdoor meetings, holding blazing torches and burning large wooden crosses.

At the peak of KKK membership in the late 1860s, Forrest commanded the activities of around one hundred thousand Klansmen throughout the South. Increasingly violent, Klansmen threatened, beat, and even murdered many blacks and black sympathizers in the region. Upset by federal government intervention against Klan activities, Forrest ordered the Invisible Empire to disband in 1869. Although some states, such as

Arkansas and North Carolina, organized local militia units to break up the Klan, most states required the help of federal troops. In 1871, Congress passed the Force Bill, authorizing the president to use federal troops against the KKK. By the following year, the KKK had virtually disappeared.

A second Klan movement swept through the United States in 1915. National membership climbed to more than three million during the early 1920s as Klansmen assumed less violent activities to promote the cause of preserving America's moral standards. Although the organization disbanded in 1944, the civil rights movement and threats of communist aggression soon fueled a third Klan movement that grew to a membership of seventeen thousand during the 1960s. Today, the Klan continues to exist in small numbers throughout the United States.

The Birth of a Newspaper Empire

· 1878 ·

H e was barely twenty years old when he borrowed $250 to buy a controlling interest in a Chattanooga newspaper. But Adolph Ochs's purchase of the *Chattanooga Times* in 1878 launched a newspaper empire that influenced journalistic standards throughout the world and paved the way for his ownership of the prestigious *New York Times.*

Adolph Simon Ochs, the son of Jewish immigrants, was born on March 12, 1858, in Cincinnati, Ohio. After the Civil War, Ochs moved to Knoxville with his family. By age eleven, he was delivering newspapers for the *Knoxville Chronicle.* Three years later, he marched into the publisher's office and announced he wanted a full-time newspaper job. The publisher quickly hired him to sweep the floors at a pay rate of twenty-five cents per week—the same pay he had received for delivering papers.

Ochs was soon promoted to "printer's devil," a position involving such tasks as cleaning the presses and running errands. Eager to advance, Ochs learned the printing trade by age sixteen. Although he enhanced his skills by moving to Kentucky and working as the assistant foreman of the composing room at the *Louisville Courier-Journal,* Ochs missed his family while living in Kentucky. Six months after leaving Knoxville, he returned to Tennessee and joined the *Knoxville Tribune.*

While working at the *Tribune,* Ochs became acquainted with a talented editorial writer named Colonel John Mac-Gowen. In 1877, the two men joined forces with a third friend to establish a Chattanooga paper, the *Dispatch.* The newspaper, however, could not survive the depressed business climate of the Reconstruction period and quickly went bankrupt. Determined to overcome his financial losses, Ochs borrowed the use of the newspaper's presses and published a city directory.

But the newspaper business was Ochs's true love. Hearing that the *Chattanooga Times* was for sale, Ochs borrowed $250 to purchase the four-page daily in 1878. The twenty-year-old convinced MacGowen to serve as editor and hired a reporter, paying his employees through a barter system by obtaining credit slips from merchants for advertising. Starting with a circulation of 250, the *Chattanooga Times* quickly increased its readership and advertising base with its reputation of quality.

Soon the newspaper was making an impressive $25,000 per year. Ochs constructed a six-story granite building with a golden dome to house his publishing business, served as one of the founders of the Southern Associated Press, and invested in a promising land deal. The land deal soured, however, leaving Ochs with debts of more than $100,000.

Because his Chattanooga newspaper was turning a profit, Ochs reasoned that ownership of two newspapers could help him pay off his debts. As he searched for a newspaper with growth potential, Ochs discovered that *The New York Times* was heading for bankruptcy. Circulation had slumped to nine thousand, and the newspaper was losing thousands of dollars each week. Ochs developed an elaborate financial plan to acquire control of the faltering paper, using borrowed money. When *The New York Times* was placed on the auction block in August 1896, Ochs was the only bidder, acquiring control of the paper for $75,000.

In contrast to the prevailing yellow journalism of the day, Ochs insisted that *The New York Times* would "give the news impartially, without fear or favor." He also created the slogan that continues to appear on the front page of the paper: "All the News That's Fit to Print." Despite a shortage of capital, Ochs refused to accept dishonest or offensive advertisements. Moreover, he cut the price of the newspaper from three cents to one cent to compete against the more sensational "penny" papers. With his high standards of editorial excellence, Ochs tripled circulation within the first year.

By 1900, Ochs had purchased a controlling interest in the newspaper and built the *Times* into an internationally respected daily. He eliminated fiction, added a Sunday magazine, introduced book reviews, and printed useful financial information. In 1904, he built new offices for the paper at Forty-second Street and Broadway on a triangular piece of land that became known as Times Square. He also owned Philadelphia newspapers from 1902 to 1912 and consolidated the two publications under the name of the *Philadelphia Public Ledger.*

Ochs served as a director of the Associated Press from 1900 until his death in 1935 in Chattanooga. Today *The New York Times* is owned by the descendants of Adolph Ochs, who started his newspaper empire from a simple Chattanooga newspaper in 1878.

The Grim Reaper's Visit to Memphis
· 1878 ·

The future seemed bright for the city of Memphis after the Civil War. Despite the turmoil of the 1860s, the population of Memphis doubled during the decade. Riverboats and railways linked Memphis to other major cities in the South, boosting commerce and luring new residents to the area. Nearly forty-eight thousand people were living in the river city—until the Grim Reaper arrived with a deadly epidemic of yellow fever, casting doom over Memphis and destroying the lives of thousands of residents.

Before Dr. Walter Reed discovered the cause of yellow fever in 1900, Americans were unaware that tiny mosquitoes transmitted the disease. The South's hot, sultry summers provided the perfect breeding grounds for mosquitoes, and little could be done to halt the spread of the fever during the nineteenth century. Moreover, southern cities along the Mississippi River were particularly vulnerable to yellow fever outbreaks, unable to prevent infected river travelers from carrying the disease from port to port.

After an outbreak of yellow fever hit the Caribbean in the summer of 1878, the disease quickly spread to New Orleans, then traveled north along the Mississippi River to claim its first Memphis victim. Kate Bionda, a woman who had served food to travelers in a small riverfront shop, dropped dead of yellow fever on August 13. Two days later, twenty-two Memphis residents had contracted the disease. When thirty-three new cases erupted on the following day, panic swept through the city. Residents hastily packed up their belongings and crowded into boats, trains, and wagons to escape the clutches of the Grim Reaper. As one survivor recalled, "On any road leading out of Memphis could be seen a procession of wagons, piled high with beds, trunks, and small furniture, carrying also the women and children."

Within ten days of Kate Bionda's death, over twenty-five thousand people had fled the city. Another thirteen hundred people took shelter in tents that had been set up by Memphis authorities on the outskirts of town. The remaining twenty thousand residents—some fourteen thousand blacks and another six thousand whites—braced themselves for the worst as the disease reached epidemic proportions.

Throughout September, nearly two hundred deaths occurred every day in Memphis. One resident described the hopelessness of the grim situation in a letter to a relative: "The fever is raging and spreading all over the city. . . . Our people are falling in every direction. . . . God help us. . . . Where will the end be?"

To aid the sick and dying, the Citizens' Relief Committee coordinated the distribution of essential supplies, such as candles, soap, food, and bedding. Religious organizations and local fraternal groups, such as the Masons, provided relief services. Some fifty Catholic nuns nursed patients throughout the city, while twenty-five priests offered comfort and last rites. But no one was immune to the disease. The chairman of the Citizens' Relief Committee died on the job, and thirty nuns and thirteen priests became victims of the plague.

The Howard Association, a philanthropic organization composed of approximately forty Memphis businessmen, recruited emergency medical workers to help victims of the epidemic. Dozens of physicians and nurses from other cities responded to the call, setting to work immediately after their arrival in Memphis. But like relief workers, medical personnel could not escape from the disease. Nurses, both male and female, suffered heavy casualties. Nearly half of the 111 physicians contracted the fever, resulting in 33 deaths.

Throughout the city, the remaining occupants prayed for the swift arrival of the first frost of the season. Although it was common knowledge that the first frost would stop the disease from spreading, no one realized that this was because the cold weather would prevent mosquito larvae from hatching and transmitting the fever. Finally, after more than sixty days of the killer epidemic, the first frost of the season arrived on October 18. Within ten days, physicians were no longer reporting new cases of the disease, and the city's board of health declared that the epidemic had officially ended. To celebrate the disappearance of the Grim Reaper, militia companies paraded down Main Street behind the local coronet band, and residents who had fled the city began returning to their homes.

By the time the disease ran its course through two hundred towns and cities along the Mississippi, Ohio, and Tennessee river valleys, yellow fever had claimed twenty thousand lives. But the worst impact was felt in Memphis. Nearly all of the six thousand whites who remained in the city contracted the disease. More than four thousand whites died, resulting in a mortality rate of almost 70 percent. Blacks, however, fared better than their white neighbors, accounting for fewer than one thousand deaths out of eleven thousand cases during the ten-week epidemic.

A new epidemic of yellow fever hit Memphis in the fall of 1879, causing nearly six hundred deaths out of two thousand cases. By 1880, the population of Memphis had dropped to thirty-three thousand, declining by almost fifteen thousand residents over the span of two years. To discourage the arrival of another epidemic, the city immediately launched programs to improve sanitation and cleanliness along the riverfront and city streets.

By 1900, Memphis had not been plagued by a yellow fever epidemic in more than a decade, and the city's population soared to one hundred thousand. Moreover, with Dr. Walter Reed's discovery of the cause of the disease, Memphis and other American cities no longer had to fear the arrival of another mosquito plague like the deadly epidemic of 1878.

The British Invasion of Tennessee

• 1880 •

Historians claim England's attempts to colonize America ended with the British surrender at Yorktown, the decisive battle of the Revolutionary War. But few people realize that some British citizens invaded American territory more than one hundred years after the Revolution. In the late 1800s, an enterprising group of Englishmen established the last British settlement in the United States—the colony of Rugby, Tennessee.

Rugby was the noble venture of Thomas Hughes, a member of the British Parliament and the noted author of *Tom Brown's School Days*. Hughes established the colony in October 1880 to provide the younger sons of English aristocrats opportunities to pursue their dreams in the New World.

Under nineteenth-century law, members of the British aristocracy bequeathed family fortunes to their eldest sons. Although other sons had no rightful claim to an inheritance, they were expected to pursue an honorable profession, such as law, medicine, or the ministry. Young lords who engaged in unacceptable occupations were doomed in the eyes of British society. But the establishment of Rugby provided England's "second sons" with the chance to pursue the trades and skills of commoners—without fear of embarrassing their families in England.

Hughes located his "New Jerusalem" on seventy-five thousand acres in Morgan County, Tennessee, deep in the heart of the Cumberland Plateau. A counselor to Queen Victoria, Hughes persuaded influential friends to finance his new enterprise by praising the beauty of the "enchanted wilderness." As a tribute to his alma mater, Hughes named the new colony "Rugby."

Undoubtedly, well-bred, well-educated British lords who took up residence in the colony experienced culture shock upon their arrival. The primitive settlement initially consisted of nothing more than a few shanties in the remote mountain terrain. Lacking customary cultural events and the comforts of home, bored colonists soon created their own lawn tennis court in the wilderness and cut a bridle path along the banks of the Clear Fork River.

After the colony's official opening in 1880, however, skilled workmen were hired to transform the remote site into an English village. Roads were cut, streets named, and buildings constructed. Victorian cottages—complete with English lawns and gardens—soon appeared, christened in the true English tradition with names such as Roslyn, Twin Oaks, and Kingston Lisle. Within a year, Rugby was home to three hundred residents and had more than a dozen structures. Interestingly, Thomas Hughes chose not to live in the colony. Eventually, Rugby boasted a large school, a church, a commissary with a town hall, a library, and an elegant inn.

Frequent reports about Rugby appeared in British newspapers, luring guests and new residents to the settlement. Rugby's Tabard Inn, the namesake of the hostelry in Chaucer's *Canterbury Tales,* provided accommodations for numerous guests who visited the colony. A replica of an English club, the Tabard Inn featured an excellent dining room, billiard tables, and croquet courts. Much to the delight of visitors, the three-story hotel prominently displayed a banister from the original Tabard Inn of Shakespeare's day.

By 1884, Rugby had more than four hundred residents. But not all residents were Englishmen. Some native East Tennessee mountaineers lived there, along with several British families and New England transplants.

Still, English customs and traditions prevailed in the Tennessee colony. Residents favored plum pudding and Worcester sauce over the local fare, and English tea was a daily ritual. At the appointed hour, men donned their starched shirts to join the ladies for tea at the Tabard Inn.

Colonists also indulged in traditional activities of the motherland by establishing their own social, musical, and sporting clubs. Residents created an amateur brass band, staged dramatic events, and participated in archery, baseball, and football clubs. Other enterprising colonists published *The Rugbeian,* the only newspaper within a five-county region.

One of the most popular features of the colony was the Thomas Hughes Free Public Library. Hughes, a success in the publishing world, with sixty-six printings of *Tom Brown's School Days,* persuaded prominent publishers to contribute literature to the Rugby library. A clapboard building with a clipped gable roof and cupola housed seven thousand volumes of British and American literature donated by publishers in honor of Hughes.

Although Hughes successfully transformed the tract of wilderness into a quaint English village, he was not as victorious in his efforts to develop an outlet for the talents of young British noblemen. Pursuits of pleasure and happiness were far more important to the young sons of British gentry than enterprise and survival. Most British colonists were "remittance men" who received healthy subsidies from home that encouraged their leisurely activities.

Worse yet, most of the colonists did not have experience and training in manual labor. Although the region had an abundance of coal and timber, Rugbeians lacked necessary skills to take advantage of the plentiful natural resources in the area.

Residents turned to other ventures in their quest to succeed in the wilderness. But a variety of attempts—a tomato canning factory, sheep raising, and brick, pottery, and dairy enterprises—all ended in disaster. Agricultural efforts failed as well, when sons of the British gentry struggled to farm the rocky, mountainous terrain.

One venture, however, resulted in temporary triumph for the colony. Banking on the natural beauty of the Appalachian Mountains, Hughes promoted the area as a health resort. Early advertisements in British publications stressed that the climate was not only free from mosquitoes and malaria, but beneficial to those suffering from asthma and bronchial disorders.

For a few years, Rugby's popularity as a tourist resort attracted travelers and vacationers from England and various regions of the United States. Visitors in "delicate health" came to the Tabard Inn to breathe the clear mountain air and drink mineral waters that supposedly had medicinal qualities.

But problems persisted in the colony. Cold winters and dry summers took their toll on the residents, fires ripped through the colony, and insufficient management contributed to squabbles over leadership and a barrage of administrative woes. A contaminated water supply—from the same well that had produced the miraculous healing waters—led to an outbreak of typhoid fever that resulted in the death of several Englishmen. Although Rugbeians quickly disinfected the Tabard Inn, boiled all drinking water, and terminated the outbreak, the event tarnished the colony's reputation as a health resort.

The residents' inability to overcome the multitude of dilemmas that plagued the settlement led to the demise of the colony in 1887. Still, many colonists remained in the region and established permanent homes along the Cumberland Plateau.

Today, reminders of Hughes's admirable endeavor linger in Morgan County. Through the efforts of the Rugby Restoration Association, the little British colony remains very much alive in nineteenth-century style. Regular worship services are still held at Christ Church, a beautiful Gothic structure constructed in 1882. Several Victorian cottages adorned with gingerbread trim and quaint gables remain in the village. And the Thomas Hughes Library, with its rich collection of original Victorian literature, today presents literally the same appearance as it did on its opening day in 1882, standing as a tribute to the last attempt at creating an English settlement on American soil.

The First Coca-Cola Bottling Company
• 1899 •

It's one of the most famous brands in the world, marketed and sold in cans and bottles around the globe. Created by Atlanta druggist Doc Pemberton in 1886, Coca-Cola quickly gained a loyal following of devoted fans during the final decade of the nineteenth century. But the "refreshing taste" of Coca-Cola reached far beyond the boundaries of Atlanta when a group of Tennesseans purchased the rights to bottle the beverage in 1899—and established Coke's first franchised bottling plant in Chattanooga.

Before the start of the twentieth century, Coca-Cola was sold exclusively at soda fountains. Local soda fountain "jerks" mixed the beverage by hand, combining the sweet brown syrup with carbonated water. The distribution arrangement satisfied Asa Candler, who purchased sole ownership of the beverage for $2,300 in 1891. Several unsuccessful attempts to bottle the drink soured Candler's opinion of bottling Coke, and he became highly protective of his product. As president of the Coca-Cola Company, Candler indicated that his company had "neither the money, nor time, nor brains, to embark in the bottling business, and there are too many folks who are not responsible, who care nothing about the reputation of what they put up, and I am afraid the name will be injured."

But a Chattanooga lawyer formed a different opinion about bottling Coke. While stationed in Cuba during the Spanish-American War of 1898, Benjamin Franklin Thomas noted the popularity of a bottled, carbonated drink known as "champagne cola." By the time he returned to Chattanooga, Thomas was determined to find a soft drink that would make a good candidate for bottling, envisioning success from "something inexpensive . . . that could be used up quickly and then repurchased." Hearing about Thomas's ambitions, Chattanoogan Sam Erwin suggested that Thomas contact his first cousin, Asa Candler, president of the Coca-Cola Company. Convinced that Coke was the right product for bottling, Thomas quickly approached a fellow Chattanooga attorney and businessman about his idea. By the summer of 1899, Joseph Brown Whitehead had agreed to join forces with Thomas as a partner in the new venture.

As the first step in establishing their new company, the two partners had to convince Candler to let them bottle the soft drink. Leery of losing control over his product, Candler initially balked at the idea. Thomas and Whitehead persisted in their dream, promising Candler that they would "make the name [Coca-Cola] better every day we conduct this business." After checking into their backgrounds, Candler finally agreed to meet with the two men at his Atlanta office. To prepare for the meeting, Thomas and Whitehead drafted a short contract for purchasing the rights to bottle Coca-Cola.

On July 21, 1899, Thomas and Whitehead presented their proposal to Candler. After reading the six-hundred-word contract, the president of the Coca-Cola Company signed the document without seeking legal counsel. In exchange for one dollar, Candler sold the exclusive rights for bottling Coca-Cola throughout most of the United States to the two Chattanoogans.

No one knows if Candler ever collected payment from Thomas and Whitehead. According to one account, Candler nonchalantly signed away the bottling rights to the two men because he was preoccupied with a migraine headache on that summer day. Another source contends that Thomas and Whitehead gained the bottling rights for a token sum because they were willing to bankroll the high costs of establishing a bottling business—ranging from $500 to $1,500 for mules, wagons, equipment, and a processing plant. Regardless, Candler apparently held little faith in the notion of bottling his product. As the two men left his office, Candler reportedly said, "If you boys fail in this undertaking, don't come back to cry on my shoulder because I have very little confidence in this bottling business."

Thomas and Whitehead could not be swayed from their vision for the company. By the fall of 1899, the partners had incorporated their business under the name of the Coca-Cola Bottling Company. About the same time, mule-drawn wagons delivered the first bottles of Coca-Cola to Chattanooga stores. And on November 12, 1899, the company placed its first advertisement in the *Chattanooga Times,* encouraging customers to "Drink a bottle of Coca-Cola—five cents at all stands, grocers, and saloons."

After establishing the first bottling company specifically for Coca-Cola in Chattanooga, Thomas and Whitehead dreamed of creating a national bottling company. Lacking the money and the manpower to cover the country, they determined that they needed additional capital to finance their dream. On December 9, 1899, Chattanooga lawyer and businessman John Thomas Lupton agreed to provide the necessary capital by purchasing half of Whitehead's shares for $2,500.

To expand their bottling operations across the country, the three businessmen decided to sell Coca-Cola bottling rights to local bottling companies throughout the nation. The trio then divided the country into two regions to effectively manage the franchises. Thomas took the western and northwestern states, inheriting the original Coca-Cola Bottling Company chartered in Tennessee. The Whitehead–Lupton team organized their half of the bottling empire as the Dixie Coca-Cola Bottling Company in Chattanooga, assuming responsibility for selling franchise rights in the southern and southwestern states.

By licensing the production and sale of Coke in bottles, the parent bottlers of Coca-Cola became an important link between the Coca-Cola Company and local bottling plants throughout the country. Through their initiative and leadership, the trio of Chattanooga businessmen not only boosted the sales of Coca-Cola in bottles, but established a successful business for bottling a beverage that would become known as "The Real Thing" to millions of Coke lovers around the globe.

Casey Jones and the Cannonball Express
· 1900 ·

"Come all you rounders, for I want you to hear
The story told of a brave engineer;
Casey Jones was the rounder's name
On a six-eight wheeler, boys, he won his fame."

The popularity of a folk ballad immortalized him in song, but "Casey Jones, the Brave Engineer" was much more than a legend. In fact, John Luther "Casey" Jones was a working railroad engineer from Jackson, Tennessee, who became an American icon through his heroic death on the Cannonball Express.

The oldest of five children, John Luther Jones was born on March 14, 1864, in southeast Missouri. At an early age, Jones moved with his family to a small Kentucky town along the Mobile and Ohio Railroad. Fascinated by the locomotives speeding through Cayce, Kentucky, the youngster dreamed of becoming a railroad engineer. By age sixteen, Jones was working as a telegraph operator for the M&O.

While working his way up the line to the positions of brakeman and fireman for the M&O, Jones moved to Jackson, Tennessee. In 1888, he switched to the Illinois Central Railroad in hopes of becoming an engineer. Two years later, Jones was promoted from fireman to engineer, working the line between Jackson and Water Valley, Mississippi.

Living in Jackson, Jones married and became the father of three children. Standing at a height of 6 feet, 4 inches, the dark-haired, gray-eyed engineer was known as a big man with a big heart. When friends discovered that Jones had been raised in Cayce, Kentucky, they dubbed him "Casey," pronouncing the nickname in the same manner as the name of the Kentucky town.

As an engineer for the Illinois Central, Casey Jones took pride in keeping his train on schedule. He garnered a reputation for pushing his engines, racing down the tracks to make up lost time or to arrive on schedule. He was also known for the distinctive whippoorwill sound of his whistle. Some individuals claimed that they set their watches by the sound of his whistle, knowing they could depend on Casey Jones to keep his train on time.

In early 1900, Jones's reputation for maintaining the railroad's schedules apparently helped him to win a bid on a new job as the engineer of a passenger train that ran between Memphis and Canton, Mississippi. As part of the Illinois Central's run between Chicago and New Orleans, the service was known by two names: the New Orleans Special and the Cannonball Express. Because the Cannonball Express offered the railroad's fastest service, Jones held a prestigious position as the train's engineer.

But disaster was looming on the evening of April 29, 1900, as Jones pulled Engine 382 into the Memphis station. After discovering that the engineer for the return trip to Canton was ill, Jones volunteered for the run. Ninety-five minutes behind schedule, Jones took the shift with fireman Sim Webb. To make up lost time, he pushed the train to the limit. By the time he approached Vaughan, Mississippi, 14 miles north of Canton, Jones was back on schedule. Little did he realize that six other trains were also scheduled to arrive in Canton about the same time.

As Jones approached the final station, he careened around a curve at 70 miles per hour. Seeing the lights of a caboose on the tracks, Webb alerted Jones to the danger up ahead. Jones ordered his fireman to jump. Staying at his post, Jones pulled back on the throttles and slowed the train to 35 miles per hour. At 3:52 A.M., his train collided with the caboose, and Casey was killed. Webb and the train's passengers survived without injuries.

Immediate controversy erupted over the exact cause of the crash and the nature of Jones's death. Although the *Jackson Sun* reported that dense fog prevented Jones from seeing the caboose until it was too late, the Illinois Central's official accident report placed sole blame on Jones for the accident. Some say Jones died with one hand on the whistle and the other on the airbrake lever. The story of Jones's heroic death became a national legend through the popularity of the folk ballad called "Casey Jones, the Brave Engineer" or simply "The Ballad of Casey Jones," composed by a fellow railroad worker, Wallace Saunders. Today, Casey Jones Village in Jackson, featuring Jones's home and a museum, is one of Tennessee's top tourist attractions.

The Lynching of Murderous Mary

·1916·

In the early days of the twentieth century, small towns welcomed the arrival of traveling circuses. Entertaining acts such as clowns and elephants offered a pleasant diversion from the daily routines of rural life. But Tennesseans witnessed something far more dramatic than an entertaining performance with the arrival of Sparks World Famous Shows in September 1916.

Like other traveling shows, the Sparks circus ventured from town to town by rail. The Carolina, Clinchfield, and Ohio Railroad line, commonly known as the Clinchfield Railroad, transported Sparks's performers, animals, and circus equipment to small towns along the Clinchfield route in Virginia and Tennessee. Sparks distributed handbills and posters to towns along the route in advance of the scheduled performances, hoping to lure large crowds to the big top. Playbills often featured the circus's lead performer, an elephant by the name of Mary. Mary was billed as "the largest living land animal on earth, 3 inches taller than Jumbo and weighing over 5 tons."

Following an evening performance in St. Paul, Virginia, on Monday, September 11, 1916, the Sparks troop boarded the train for an overnight journey to Kingsport, Tennessee. As soon as the train arrived in Kingsport on Tuesday morning, circus roustabouts scurried to set up the big top. A large crowd arrived for the matinee performance, jamming into wooden bleachers under the huge circus tent.

After the matinee, circus trainers led a parade of five elephants down Center Street, one of the town's main thoroughfares. Trainers rode on each elephant, carrying sticks to keep the animals under control as they worked their way toward a watering hole on Carter Street. Mary, the largest of the herd, took the lead, her tail entwined with the trunk of the animal that lumbered behind her. Fascinated, Kingston residents gathered along the sides of the wide street to watch the spectacle. Little did they realize that Mary's trainer, Walter "Red" Eldridge, had never ridden the beast until the start of the parade. Eldridge, a drifter, had reportedly joined the circus in St. Paul, Virginia, on the previous day.

The parade proceeded peacefully until Mary paused at the sight of several pigs munching on a watermelon rind on the side of the road. To keep the parade moving, Eldridge prodded the elephant with his stick. But Mary ignored the trainer and reached for the rind with her trunk. The pigs promptly scurried away just as the procession of elephants came to a halt. Eldridge whacked his stick across Mary again, hitting her sharply on the side of the head. Suddenly, the elephant wrapped her trunk around the trainer, lifted him into the air, and hurled him through the side of a wooden soft drink stand. Then she calmly walked over the man and crushed him with her foot.

Between the blares of the frightened elephants and the screams of terrified spectators, a local blacksmith bolted from his shop with a pistol in hand. Although the blacksmith fired five shots at Mary, the bullets failed to pierce the beast's tough hide. As roustabouts struggled to gain control over the animal, the crowd began to chant, "Kill the elephant! Kill the elephant!"

Charlie Sparks, the circus owner, arrived on the scene just as his workers regained control over Mary. Although Sparks probably realized that Mary's demise could be accomplished by a single shot through the elephant's ear canal, he opted to remain silent. Undoubtedly, Sparks did not welcome the idea of losing one of his most valuable assets. With a value of about eight thousand dollars, Mary represented a substantial financial investment for the circus.

Despite the tragedy, Sparks did not cancel the evening performance in Kingsport. The show proceeded as scheduled, and the town's residents turned out in full force for the event. Mary performed with the rest of the elephants, garnering a great deal of attention from an audience that was eager to see the killer creature. After the show, the circus packed up and boarded the train for an overnight journey to Erwin, Tennessee.

But the news of Eldridge's violent death spread like wildfire throughout the region. By the time the circus pulled into Erwin the next morning, two mayors from neighboring towns had banned Mary from appearing in upcoming performances. Moreover, rumors about the dangers of "Murderous Mary" were sweeping through the streets of Erwin. When the town's two thousand residents heard the false rumor that Mary had murdered as many as fifteen men, many suggested that the animal should be hanged for committing such atrocious crimes. Others speculated that Charlie Sparks was guilty by association, assuming that the circus owner had been fully aware of Mary's murderous past.

In truth, Sparks may have suspected that Mary was capable of murder when he acquired the animal for his show. Traditionally, circuses did not sell an elephant unless the beast had displayed violent or unusual behavior. Like other circus operators who acquired elephants with a history of troublesome behavior, Sparks probably renamed the elephant to give her a new identity and to conceal her past history from the unsuspecting public. Another theory suggests that Eldridge struck Mary's abscessed tooth with his stick, causing the normally subdued elephant to become wild with pain.

The fury evoked by Mary's murderous act in Kingsport convinced Sparks that the elephant had to be destroyed. Intrigued by the idea of hanging the elephant, Sparks quickly discussed the possibility with railroad employees. The men decided that a boom on the railroad's derrick car, normally used for hoisting and lowering heavy loads of freight, could serve as a makeshift gallows for the elephant. Convinced that the act of lynching an elephant would generate free publicity for the circus, Sparks agreed to the plan. Within a few hours, he invited the public to witness the hanging of an elephant in the Clinchfield Railroad yards immediately after the matinee performance.

An estimated crowd of three thousand arrived at the railroad yards to witness the event. Roustabouts looped a chain around Mary's neck and secured the end of the chain around the boom of the derrick car. Then railroad workers adjusted the controls to reel in the chain. Just as the boom and chain lifted Mary into the air, the cable snapped. The elephant plunged to the ground with a thud, prompting screams from the crowd. But the killer elephant remained frozen, numbed by a broken hip from the fall. After roustabouts attached a heavier chain around the animal's neck, railroad workers resumed their task. Once again, the chain tightened around Mary's neck, and the boom lifted the animal into the air. Mary struggled for a few moments, then fell limp from suffocation.

Railroad laborers and circus roustabouts buried Mary in a grave that was "as big as a barn," according to one witness. A photograph of Mary's hanging, reportedly snapped by a Clinchfield employee, provides evidence of the lynching of the killer elephant in Erwin, Tennessee, on September 13, 1916.

Winning the Right to Vote for Women
· 1920 ·

The fragrant scent of roses wafted through Tennessee's Capitol Hill on the morning of August 18, 1920, mingling with the sense of breathless anticipation that hovered through the crowd. After weeks of heated political debate, Tennessee legislators were ready to vote on an issue that would affect American women from all walks of life: the right to vote in the 1920 presidential election.

One year earlier, Congress had approved the suffrage amendment to the U.S. Constitution, granting women the right to vote. Congress then sent the amendment to the states for approval, requiring ratification from three-fourths of the forty-eight states. Over the course of the following year, thirty-five states ratified the amendment. But in June 1920, progress came to a dead halt. Needing only one more state to complete the ratification process, suffragists were dismayed when Delaware unexpectedly defeated the amendment, making it the only state north of the Mason-Dixon line to deny ratification. To make matters worse, most of the southern states had already defeated ratification, and no other state was slated to hold a legislative session before the November 1920 election.

Tensions mounted as Connecticut, Vermont, and Florida refused to call their legislatures into session to consider ratification. Then North Carolina legislators defeated the amendment, and the focus shifted to Tennessee. Could the Volunteer State help the suffrage cause?

With encouragement from state governors and President Woodrow Wilson, Tennessee Governor Albert H. Roberts called a special session of the Tennessee legislature to consider ratification of the suffrage amendment. By the time the state legislature convened on August 9, the debate over the right of women to vote in the November election rested solely in the hands of Tennessee legislators.

Suffragists from across the nation flocked to Nashville for the event, including Carrie Chapman Catt, head of the National American Women Suffrage Association. As legislators arrived in the state capital for the special session, suffragists promptly greeted the state politicians with boutonnieres of yellow roses. In contrast to the suffragists' yellow symbol, antisuffragists adopted the American Beauty red rose as their emblem. Soon members of Tennessee's all male, all white legislation were sporting boutonnieres of red or yellow roses to display their support or opposition of the suffrage cause.

The special session attracted national interest, filling local hotels to capacity. Antisuffrage liquor lobbyists opened a hospitality suite on the eighth floor of the Hermitage Hotel, dispensing whiskey around the clock. Rumors of bribes and questionable behavior flowed through Nashville as lobbyists worked feverishly, pollsters tallied votes, and women vied for seats in the House gallery during the legislative sessions. One observer later noted, "The Battle of Nashville in 1864 was a five o'clock tea in comparison with this one."

On the first day of the special session, Governor Roberts addressed the packed galleries, urging ratification "in justice to the womanhood of America." Four days later, the state senate debated the issue for only three hours before passing the resolution with twenty-five ayes, four nays, and two not voting. The resolution was then passed to the House for consideration.

After several days of debate, the House scheduled a vote for Wednesday morning, August 18. As suffragists in white dresses with yellow sashes crowded into the House chamber, yellow banners streamed between the chamber's tall columns. Although the House speaker promptly moved to kill the amendment by tabling it, the motion failed on a tie vote of forty-eight to forty-eight. As the house prepared to vote again on the original motion, the suffragists held their breath. They still needed one more vote to have a majority of forty-nine.

No one dreamed that the state's youngest legislator, Harry Burn, would dare to switch his vote. At age twenty-four, the McMinn County representative was wearing a red rose in his lapel, signifying his support against ratification. But no one could see the letter tucked into Burn's pocket.

That morning, Burn had received a letter from his mother, Mrs. J. L. Burn of Niota, Tennessee. Reading newspaper reports of the special session, she had been disappointed that her son had not taken a stand.

Dear Son: Hurrah, and vote for suffrage! Don't keep them in doubt. I notice some of the speeches against. They were bitter. I have been watching to see how you stood, but I have not noticed anything yet. Don't forget to be a good boy and help Mrs. Catt put the "rat" in ratification. Your Mother.

As the roll call proceeded, Burn quietly changed his vote in support of ratification. The young legislator's decision enabled the state House of Representatives to pass the resolution with a simple majority of a single vote—and made Tennessee the pivotal state needed to complete ratification of the national "Susan B. Anthony Amendment."

Realizing the resolution had passed by a vote of forty-nine to forty-seven, women screamed, wept, and danced for joy. The uproar drowned out the clerk's announcement that the

House had approved the resolution. As a shower of yellow rose petals floated down from the galleries, suffragist legislators ripped off their yellow boutonnieres and threw them into the air.

The day after the vote, Burn stood in the House chamber to explain his decision to change sides. "I know that a mother's advice is always safest for her boy to follow, and my mother wanted me to vote for ratification," he said.

With Tennessee's ratification of the Nineteenth Amendment, votes for women became the law of the land. On August 26, 1920, the Nineteenth Amendment to the U.S. Constitution took effect, proclaiming that the right of citizens "to vote shall not be denied or abridged by the United States or by any State on account of sex."

The Scopes "Monkey" Trial

• 1925 •

O n the morning of July 13, 1925, the eyes of the world focused on the Rhea County Courthouse in the small town of
Dayton, Tennessee, about 35 miles northeast of Chattanooga.
With the pounding of the gavel, the Honorable John T.
Raulston marked the beginning of one of the most intriguing
trials of the century, a trial that would represent a debate between religion and science, faith and reason.

The small courtroom was filled to capacity on that sweltering summer morning. Waiting for the courtroom battle to
begin, the crowd flowed onto the courthouse lawn and spilled
into the streets. The area surrounding the courthouse resem-
bled a country fair as vendors set up booths to hawk food and
souvenirs. A local teacher was set to be tried for violating a
new state law, and two of the nation's most brilliant legal minds
were ready to debate a case that would be known as the "Mon-
key Trial."

A few months earlier, Tennessee had joined forces with
five other southern states to pass a law that prohibited the
teaching of evolution in the classroom. As word spread about
the new legislation, the American Civil Liberties Union (ACLU)
offered free legal support to any teacher who was willing to
challenge the law in court.

When news of the ACLU's backing reached Dayton, several Rhea County residents gathered at F. E. Robinson's Drug Store to discuss the controversial statute. The new law was already gaining a great deal of attention from the press, and local residents were eager for the chance to obtain international publicity for their small town. All they needed was a local teacher who had violated the law and who was willing to challenge it in court. Within a few days, the residents convinced John T. Scopes to test the new law. A mild-mannered football coach and substitute biology teacher at Rhea County High School, Scopes agreed.

On May 7, 1925, Scopes was arrested for suspicion of teaching in a public classroom a scientific theory that denied the story of divine creation. A preliminary hearing was held three days later, and Scopes was indicted for committing a misdemeanor. The group from Robinson's Drug Store called the *Chattanooga News* to report the arrest, setting into motion more publicity for the town of Dayton. By the time the trial began in mid-July, the rural town was overflowing with people, including more than twenty Western Union operators and scores of reporters. Even WGN, a Chicago radio station, was on hand to cover the trial, marking the nation's first live radio broadcast of a jury trial.

The ACLU provided financial support for Scopes's defense, and Clarence Darrow became his attorney. A brilliant man who had served as a defense lawyer for nearly two thousand cases, Darrow was prepared to center the case on Charles Darwin's theory of evolution. Tom Stewart and William Jennings Bryan, a three-time presidential candidate and former secretary of state to President Woodrow Wilson, represented the state's case. A staunch fundamentalist and religious leader, Bryan was an eloquent orator who had spoken against the theory of evolution in a campaign of tent revivals across the state.

As Darrow entered the courtroom, he intended to call expert witnesses to argue the case of evolution as valid educational material. But Judge Raulston quickly shattered Darrow's plans by denying scientific testimony about evolution. In an unusual and theatrical move, Darrow called on the testimony of one witness: one of the prosecutors for the case, William Jennings Bryan.

Darrow relentlessly grilled Bryan on his literal interpretation of the Bible, casting a spell over the courtroom with his brilliant arguments. Furthermore, he discredited Bryan's testimony by drawing links between the teachings of religious leaders and the theory of evolution. He also crushed Bryan's hopes of presenting a persuasive closing argument when Judge Raulston granted his request for an immediate verdict.

Twelve days after the trial opened, the jury reached a verdict in only eight minutes. Scopes was found guilty as charged and fined $100. Although Scopes's conviction upheld the law, the fundamentalist cause received a severe blow from Darrow's public humiliation of Bryan. Moreover, the amount of Scopes's fine was the bare minimum required by law.

Five days after the jury's verdict, Bryan died in Dayton from complications of diabetes. Scopes soon left Dayton to study geology in Chicago, later working for an oil company in Venezuela and a Louisiana gas company. Clarence Darrow continued to practice law, dazzling juries with his brilliant defense tactics.

On January 14, 1927, the Tennessee Supreme Court reversed the decision of the lower court. The court's ruling, however, was based on a technicality, leaving the constitutional issue unchallenged. Although the antievolution law remained on the books, the statute was not enforced. Evolution continued to be taught in public schools until 1968, when the U.S. Supreme Court overturned a similar Arkansas law. Ironically, before his death in 1970, John Scopes denied that he had ever taught or mentioned the theory of evolution in the classroom.

America's First Guide Dogs for the Blind

• 1929 •

Trained guide dogs increase the mobility and independence of their owners, allowing thousands of blind Americans to travel safely through today's busy streets. But trained guide dogs were not available in the United States until a blind Tennessean convinced a wealthy kennel owner to establish the nation's first guide dog school, The Seeing Eye, in Nashville during 1929.

The founder of The Seeing Eye, Dorothy Eustis, was a Pennsylvania native. After moving to Switzerland during the early 1920s, she established a kennel and experimented with selective breeding of dogs. Known for breeding German shepherds with high intelligence, Eustis developed a training program for the dogs. Canine graduates of Eustis's kennel assisted the Swiss Army and numerous metropolitan police departments throughout Europe, performing such tasks as delivering messages.

In 1927, Eustis visited a school in Germany that trained German shepherds as guides for blind veterans of World War I. Deeply impressed by the training program, Eustis wrote an article about the school, "The Seeing Eye." The article appeared in the November 5, 1927, issue of the *Saturday Evening Post.*

When Morris S. Frank heard about the article, he immediately penned a letter to Eustis. A resident of Nashville, Morris had lost his vision from an accident. "Thousands of blind like me abhor being dependent on others," he wrote. "Help me and I will help them. Train me and I will bring back my dog and show people here how a blind man can be absolutely on his own."

In response to Frank's letter, Eustis selected and trained a dog for the young Tennessean. In 1928, Frank traveled to Switzerland and learned to work with Buddy, a German shepherd from Eustis's kennels. Back in the United States, he crisscrossed the country with Buddy, demonstrating the dog's abilities to guide him safely through city streets. On one occasion, a reporter challenged Frank and Buddy to cross a busy street in New York City. Frank later recalled the experience:

We entered a street so noisy it was almost like entering a wall of sound. Buddy went about four paces and halted. A deafening roar and a rush of hot air told me a tremendous truck was swooshing past so near that Buddy could have lifted her nose and touched it. She moved forward again to the ear-splitting clangor, stopped, backed up and started again. I lost all sense of direction and surrendered myself entirely to her.

I shall never forget the next three minutes. Ten-ton trucks rocketing past, cabs blowing their horns in our ears, drivers shouting at us. One fellow yelled, "You damned fool, do you want to get killed?"

When we finally got to the other side and I realized what a really magnificent job she had done, I leaned over and gave Buddy a great big hug and told her what a good girl she was. "She sure is a good girl," exclaimed a voice at my elbow—one of the photographers. "I had to come over in a cab, and some of the fellows who tried to cross with you are still back on the other side."

Frank and Buddy received wide publicity, generating even more inquiries from blind Americans about the use of guide dogs. As a result, Eustis returned to the United States to establish The Seeing Eye, America's first guide dog school, in Frank's home city of Nashville. In February 1929, The Seeing Eye conducted its first class in Nashville, training two students to work with guide dogs. By the end of the year, seventeen blind students had achieved new levels of independence with their Seeing Eye dogs.

In 1984, the Walt Disney Company produced a television movie based on the life of Morris Frank. Starring actor Timothy Bottoms as Frank, *Love Leads the Way* centered on Frank's troubles functioning in the world after losing his sight from a boxing accident. The movie not only demonstrated Frank's quest to obtain a guide dog from Dorothy Eustis in Switzerland, but his fight to remove the legal barriers that prevented him from taking his companion into public buildings and businesses.

With Eustis providing funds from her personal fortune, The Seeing Eye organization moved to Morristown, New Jersey, in 1931. Today, the organization not only breeds, raises, and trains guide dogs, but trains instructors for the dogs and instructs blind people how to work with their new companions. Since the founding of the organization in Nashville in 1929, The Seeing Eye has matched more than 12,500 trained dogs with nearly 6,000 blind individuals from every state in America and every Canadian province.

The Girl Who Struck Out Babe Ruth

• 1931 •

A crowd of four thousand baseball fans gathered at Chattanooga's Engel Stadium on April 2, 1931, eagerly waiting to see the New York Yankees play an exhibition game against the hometown team, the Chattanooga Lookouts. But the spectators who filled the stadium on that spring afternoon observed much more than a fleeting glimpse of such baseball greats as Babe Ruth and Lou Gehrig. As soon as a seventeen-year-old girl stepped up to the pitcher's mound, the crowd witnessed a moment of baseball history.

A few days before the game, Joe Engel, owner of Chattanooga's Class AA minor league team, offered a contract to a young girl who had caught his attention while polishing her pitching skills at a baseball camp in Atlanta. Virne Beatrice "Jackie" Mitchell quickly accepted Engel's offer, becoming only the second female to sign a minor league contract. While living in her native Memphis, Mitchell had been encouraged by her father, an optometrist, to play baseball, reportedly developing her talents under the instruction of a neighbor who later pitched for the Brooklyn Dodgers. After moving to Chattanooga with her family, Mitchell continued to show promise on the baseball diamond as a member of the Engelettes, a women's baseball team managed by her father and supported by Engel. Moreover, she demonstrated her talents by striking out nine men in succession during an amateur game.

Her unusual pitching style immediately caught the attention of the local press. "She uses an odd, side-armed delivery, and puts both speed and curve on the ball," reported the *Chattanooga News*. "Her greatest asset, however, is control. She can place the ball where she pleases, and her knack at guessing the weakness of a batter is uncanny. . . . She doesn't hope to enter the big show this season, but she believes that with careful training she may soon be the first woman to pitch in the big leagues."

Mitchell, however, did not have to wait to participate in a major league game. Less than a week after she signed the minor league contract, the New York Yankees stopped in Chattanooga on their way home from spring training for an exhibition game with the Lookouts. Word quickly spread that Engel intended to pit Mitchell against the legendary Babe Ruth. Headlines on the sports page of *The New York Times* revealed, "Ruth Will Face Girl Pitching Today: Home Run King Alarmed by Prospect." According to the article, Ruth sneered at the prospect of female athletes invading his beloved sport. "I don't know what's going to happen if they begin to let women in baseball. Of course, they will never make good. Why? Because they are too delicate. It would kill them to play ball every day," Ruth said.

Although the New York team was scheduled to play the Lookouts on April Fool's Day, rain forced officials to postpone the match until half past two on the following afternoon. Thousands of fans, scores of reporters, and even a newsreel camera operator crowded into the local baseball stadium. Mitchell, dressed in a baggy, custom-made white uniform, joined her teammates in the dugout as the starting pitcher for the Lookouts, Clyde Barfoot, stepped onto the pitcher's mound. His opening pitches resulted in a double and a single, and Lookouts manager Bert Niehoff signaled for Mitchell to replace Barfoot.

At that moment, Babe Ruth stepped into the batter's box.

The crowd "cheered the local girl athlete heartily as she faced the Sultan of Swat," *The New York Times* later reported. After tipping his hat to Mitchell, Ruth swung at the first pitch and missed. Then he passed on two balls, swung at another pitch—and missed again. The rookie's next pitch proved to be Ruth's undoing, cutting right over the heart of the plate. "Strike three!" yelled the umpire. "You're out!" Newsreels reveal that Ruth kicked the dirt, yelled at the umpire, slammed down his bat, and stomped back to the dugout.

Then Lou Gehrig stepped up to bat. Mitchell hurled back her arm and pitched the ball across the plate. Gehrig hit nothing but air. After two more strikes, the crowd jumped up and cheered. Mitchell had struck out the Sultan of Swat and the Iron Horse—back to back.

After a standing ovation of several minutes, Mitchell walked the next Yankee, Tony Lazzari. The Lookouts' manager quickly pulled her out of the game, replacing her with Barfoot. At the bottom of the ninth inning, the Yankees claimed victory with a score of 14 to 4. But the final results paled in comparison to Mitchell's moment of glory. Her ability to strike out two of baseball's greatest players earned the young woman a permanent place in baseball history.

Unfortunately, Mitchell's shining moment did not pave the way for a bright future in sports. Within days of the game, baseball commissioner Kennesaw Mountain Landis canceled Mitchell's contract, claiming that professional baseball was too strenuous to be played by women. Furthermore, critics questioned the validity of the event. Did Ruth and Gehrig strike out on purpose? Many believed Engel had staged the match as a publicity stunt to increase ticket sales and to draw attention to his team. Others pointed out that Ruth's display of anger was proof of his surprise at Mitchell's pitching abilities.

Regardless of the arguments, Mitchell proved that she was an exceptional female pitcher during her brief encounter with professional baseball. Restricted from the minor leagues,

Mitchell later signed with a men's amateur team and continued to play in women's leagues and exhibition games. By the age of twenty-three, Mitchell had retired from baseball to work in her father's optometry office. After her marriage to Eugene Gilbert, she settled into a quiet, private life in Chattanooga. Back in the spotlight during her later years, she threw out the first ball on the Lookouts' opening day in 1982. Her sporting accomplishments were also recognized at an Atlanta Braves game in 1985, two years before her death in Chattanooga.

The Secret
Oak Ridge Project
· 1943 ·

It was one of America's most daring experiments, a project
that not only affected millions of lives, but changed the course
of history. The Manhattan Project, as it was codenamed, operated under shrouds of secrecy during World War II in the hills
of Tennessee. But the world learned about the secret project in
the summer of 1945, when the first atomic bombs exploded
over the Japanese cities of Hiroshima and Nagasaki.

In 1939, Germany's discovery of fission—the splitting of
an atomic nucleus that triggers the release of large amounts of
energy—placed pressure on the United States to develop
atomic weapons. American scientists quickly realized that additional fission research and development held the possibility
of producing an explosive atomic device of enormous size and
power. With rapid advancement in the fission field by German
scientists, some American scientists feared that Germany could
be the first country to develop an atomic weapon. And no one
wanted to risk the chance of placing an atomic bomb in the
hands of Adolf Hitler.

After being informed that the Nazis were up to something
that could be devastating for the United States, scientist Albert
Einstein penned a letter to President Franklin D. Roosevelt. His
letter not only warned Roosevelt of the dangers, but asked the
president to initiate fission research in the United States before

German scientists could develop an atomic weapon. Although Roosevelt appointed a committee to study the development of experimental weapons, progress lagged until the Japanese attack on Pearl Harbor in December 1941. America's involvement in the war created a new sense of urgency to push forward with the development project.

In 1942, Roosevelt assigned the management of uranium and plutonium plant construction and nuclear weapons production to the United States Army. In turn, the army delegated the project to the Manhattan Engineer District in New York City. The deputy chief of the Army Corps of Engineers, Brigadier General Leslie Groves, served as the commander of the "Manhattan Project."

After studying potential sites that would be suitable for the development of an atomic bomb, Groves selected a 59,000-acre tract in the remote hills of eastern Tennessee. Situated between the small towns of Clinton and Kingston in Anderson and Roane counties, the isolated location seemed ideal for the secret project. Deep in the heart of the nation, the inland site provided a safe harbor from the threat of coastal attacks by either Japan or Germany. Moreover, the Clinch River bordered the site, offering accessibility to an abundant supply of electrical power from the Tennessee Valley Authority for the pilot production plants.

To acquire the property from residents, the Army Corps of Engineers obtained a "declaration of taking" from the Knoxville federal court, paving the way for securing clear titles to the land by court condemnation. The small, rural farming communities of Wheat, Elza, Scarboro, and Robertsville vanished as the army purchased the land holdings of about a thousand families in the area, forcing nearly four thousand individuals to relocate. Existing structures were demolished or converted to use for storage, meetings, and experiments.

Then Groves selected experienced industrial contractors such as DuPont to build and operate the production plants. In early 1943, the DuPont Corporation began the process of clearing the site, installing utility systems, building wooden structures, and bordering the entire site with fences and gates. By late summer, 150 buildings had been completed. Moreover, work progressed rapidly on three large facilities for producing fissionable material for the atomic bombs that would eventually doom Hiroshima and Nagasaki.

As the project developed, thousands of new residents moved to the area. Along with construction and service workers, the project attracted the nation's best scientists and engineers from the academic and business communities. New houses and dormitories sprang up in the area, which evolved into a new community known as Oak Ridge. By the summer of 1943, forty-two thousand workers were employed at the Tennessee research and development facility known as Clinton Laboratories. Sixty-six thousand workers were employed by 1944, seventy-five thousand by the following year. Within the short span of two years, Oak Ridge exploded with new residents, growing from an isolated farming region into the fifth largest city in Tennessee.

Although many top scientists at Clinton Laboratories must have realized that the Oak Ridge complex had been built to develop atomic payloads for the United States and its allies, the true purpose of the project remained a secret to most employees. In fact, the majority of workers did not realize the accomplishments of Clinton Laboratories until American forces dropped the world's first atomic bombs over Hiroshima on August 6, 1945, and over Nagasaki three days later.

With the successful completion of the laboratory's mission, the population of Oak Ridge dropped by half between 1945 and 1946. Clinton Laboratories continued to thrive under the name of Oak Ridge National Laboratory, working on multiple projects related to energy. Today, Martin Marietta Energy Systems, Inc., a private corporation, manages the government institution, which continues to operate on its original site and houses the world's oldest nuclear reactor. The laboratory works with universities and industrial firms in the fields of science and technology, serving as a global research center on energy, environmental issues, and basic science and technology. It is also the home of the Department of Energy's largest and most diverse laboratory. Built from an urgent need to develop atomic weapons during World War II, Oak Ridge National Laboratory now operates as one of the world's premier scientific research centers.

From Memphis to Stardom

• 1954 •

When he entered a Memphis recording studio to record his first song, the nineteen-year-old truck driver was unknown to the music industry. But his intriguing voice and appealing stage presence quickly captured the hearts of music lovers around the globe. Within a short time, the young man from Memphis had become known throughout the world as the legendary Elvis Presley.

Born on January 8, 1935, in a two-room house in Tupelo, Mississippi, Elvis Aron Presley was the son of Vernon and Gladys Presley. His twin brother, Jessie Garon, was stillborn, leaving Elvis to grow up as an only child. In 1948, the Presleys moved to Memphis. Living in public housing and low-rent homes, the family struggled to make ends meet. While attending Humes High School in Memphis, Presley worked at odd jobs to help support himself and his family.

Soon after his high school graduation in 1953, Presley dropped by a local recording studio. Curious to hear the sound of his voice on a recording, the teenager made a demo record as a belated birthday present for his mother. When he returned to Sun Studios to make a second demo in early 1954, the sound of his voice caught the attention of Sam Phillips, the studio owner. Phillips invited Presley back to the studio for a recording session with several local musicians.

On July 5, 1954, Presley cut his first commercial record, "That's All Right, Mama," at Sun Studios in Memphis. "That's All Right," backed by "Blue Moon of Kentucky," became the first of five singles recorded by Presley for the Sun label. With the initial release of his records, Presley began to perform in small clubs throughout the South. During the weekdays, he worked as a delivery truck driver for Crown Electric Company.

Presley ended his short stint as a truck driver when his musical career took off like a rocket. Requests for Presley's songs poured into local radio stations, and the young singer's popularity soared with each new record. By November 1955, Presley had signed his first contract with RCA Records. The contract incorporated the sale of his Sun contract to RCA, including his five Sun singles and unreleased Sun material. During Presley's first few recording sessions for RCA in Nashville, he worked with the Jordanaires, a popular country and gospel singing group. Soon the Jordanaires began touring with Presley.

Throughout 1956, Presley's popularity continued, extending far beyond the boundaries of Memphis and the South. Each of his records during the year—five singles and two albums—topped the music charts. The singer performed on popular national television programs such as *The Ed Sullivan Show, The Milton Berle Show,* and *The Steve Allen Show,* thrilling young audiences with his unique sound and suggestive gyrations. He also launched a successful movie career with his first film, *Love Me Tender.* By the end of the year, Presley had become the hottest sensation in the entertainment world, gaining international fame.

Although Presley's fame and fortune allowed him to live anywhere in the world, the singing sensation chose to remain in Memphis. In 1957, Presley purchased a two-story, Memphis mansion large enough to also accommodate the needs of his parents, his maternal grandmother, and himself. Known as Graceland, the mansion served as Presley's home for the remainder of his life.

Despite his celebrity status, Presley temporarily set aside his musical career in 1958 to serve his country as a member of the armed forces. After his induction into the United States Army at the Memphis Draft Board, Private Presley entered basic training at Fort Hood, Texas. While stationed in Germany, Presley met a young woman, Priscilla Beaulieu, who would later become his wife. Discharged from the army with the rank of sergeant in 1960, he immediately returned to Memphis and resumed his successful recording and film career.

During the 1960s, he became one of Hollywood's biggest stars while continuing to release top-selling albums and records. Although Presley conducted all of his recording sessions in Nashville and Hollywood throughout the decade, he returned to his roots in 1969 by cutting several records at American Sound Studios in Memphis. The all-night marathon sessions there resulted in two albums and four hit singles, including "In the Ghetto" and "Kentucky Rain."

Throughout Presley's career, Memphis charities benefited from the singer's generosity. Every Christmas season, Presley donated money to more than fifty local charities, giving back to the community that had launched his phenomenal career. In honor of the hometown hero, the city of Memphis officially changed the name of the street location of Presley's residence in 1971, renaming a portion of Highway 51 South as Elvis Presley Boulevard. Five years later, Presley recorded a top-selling country album called *From Elvis Presley Boulevard, Memphis, Tennessee* from the den of his home at Graceland, using mobile recording equipment from RCA Records.

All in all, Elvis Presley starred in over thirty movies; achieved gold, platinum, or multiplatinum sales of more than 150 different albums and singles; and was essentially at the epicenter of the creation of rock and roll. A member of the Rock and Roll Hall of Fame and the Country Music Hall of Fame, he not only introduced the world to a new era of music but became a leading influence on pop culture of the time.

Not even death could erase Presley's mark on the world. Following a late-night visit to the dentist, Presley returned to Graceland on the morning of August 16, 1977. Retreating into his master suite, Presley intended to rest for an evening flight to Maine for a scheduled concert. By late morning, the singer had died of heart failure. Shocked fans around the world mourned the loss of the beloved entertainer, refusing to part with their memories of the man and his music.

Today, Elvis Presley remains one of the nation's most legendary figures. His mansion, Graceland, attracts more than six hundred thousand visitors each year. Named to the National Register of Historic Places in 1991, Graceland is one of the most visited homes in America. Moreover, Presley's recordings and films continue to enjoy popularity around the world. With more than one billion record sales, Presley ranks as the top-selling artist in the history of the recording industry. From the beginning of his musical career at a Memphis recording studio, Presley achieved legendary stardom that continues to be remembered and celebrated by millions of fans across the globe.

The Assassination of Martin Luther King Jr.

• 1968 •

Known for his eloquent, passionate pleas for equal treatment of black Americans, Dr. Martin Luther King Jr. emerged as the leader of the civil rights movement during the 1960s. An advocate of nonviolence and civil disobedience, King urged his followers to pursue the civil rights movement in a peaceful manner. Ironically, the young Baptist minister who promoted the peaceful pursuit of equal rights became the victim of a violent death on April 4, 1968, in Memphis, Tennessee.

Born on January 15, 1929, in Atlanta, Georgia, King was a third-generation Baptist preacher who earned a doctorate from Boston University. King first captured the national spotlight in the mid-1950s while serving as the pastor of Dexter Avenue Baptist Church in Montgomery, Alabama. After Rosa Parks refused to surrender her seat to a white passenger on a Montgomery bus, King stepped forward to lead a black activist group, the Montgomery Improvement Association, in a boycott of the city's transit system. He later became a national public figure as the founder of the Southern Christian Leadership Conference, promoting nonviolent tactics to achieve equal rights for blacks.

A persuasive public speaker with charisma and influence, King served as a major contributor to the success of the civil rights movement and received the Nobel Peace Prize in 1964. He frequently organized marches and demonstrations, urging peaceful support of civil rights.

In the spring of 1968, King traveled to Memphis to demonstrate his support of a strike by the city's sanitation workers. Criticized for his plans to stay at a Holiday Inn owned by whites, King changed his accommodations to the Lorraine Motel, a facility with black ownership. Located in an economically deprived area of Memphis, the motel offered few security measures. The entrance to King's second-floor room, situated at the rear of the building, opened onto a balcony with an unobstructed view of the motel's swimming pool.

Heading for dinner on the evening of April 4, King stepped from his room at the Lorraine Motel at 6:01 P.M. Just as he leaned over the balcony railing to speak to his chauffeur, a single shot from a high-powered rifle blasted through the air. The shot mortally wounded King. In the midst of the commotion, one of King's aides pointed to a neighboring boardinghouse, indicating that the shot had been fired from a bathroom window.

An investigation by the Federal Bureau of Investigation indicated that James Earl Ray, an escapee from the Missouri State Penitentiary, was the prime suspect in King's murder. Ray immediately fled Memphis, traveling to Toronto, London, Portugal, and back to London. Before boarding a plane to Belgium, Ray was arrested at London's Heathrow Airport on June 8, 1968.

Back in Memphis, Ray pleaded guilty to King's murder on March 10, 1969. With his confession, Ray forfeited his right to a jury trial and received a sentence of ninety-nine years in prison. He later recanted his confession, indicating that King's murder was the work of a conspiracy. Ray offered little evidence to support the claim, however, and his attempts to obtain a jury trial were never successful. His escape from Tennessee's Brushy Mountain Prison in June 1977 captured national attention; Ray remained at large for fifty-four hours until he was captured in a massive manhunt. Several civil rights leaders, including members of King's family, supported Ray's requests for a jury trial during his later years. Ray died on April 23, 1998, in Nashville.

In memory of Dr. Martin Luther King Jr. and his work in the civil rights movement, Congress voted to observe a national holiday in his honor. Since 1986, Americans have observed the third Monday in January as Martin Luther King Day, commemorating the birthday of the young Baptist minister who was murdered at the age of thirty-nine in Memphis, Tennessee.

The World's Fair
· 1982 ·

Since their inception, world fairs have featured special exhibits and demonstrations to showcase the highlights and advancements of the nations of the world. The 1982 World's Fair was no exception, attracting large crowds to an international energy exposition in the host city of Knoxville, Tennessee.

A group of Knoxville businesspeople initially entertained the idea of hosting a world fair during the mid-1970s. As the headquarters for the Tennessee Valley Authority, Knoxville seemed like an ideal location for hosting a world fair with an energy theme. Moreover, the city had close connections to other major energy sources, such as Appalachian coal mines and Oak Ridge National Laboratory.

In 1976, the group established the Knoxville International Energy Exposition, Inc. (KIEE). As a nonprofit, private organization, KIEE was dedicated to establishing an international exposition in Knoxville. Working with the theme "Energy Turns the World," KIEE presented a proposal to the Bureau of International Expositions in Paris, France. On April 27, 1977, the bureau unanimously approved the proposal. By late 1978, President Jimmy Carter had issued a proclamation authorizing the secretary of state to invite foreign countries to the event.

To prepare a site for the 1982 World's Fair, the city of Knoxville acquired a seventy-three-acre tract between downtown Knoxville and the University of Tennessee campus. Using bonds to finance the undertaking, the city improved the grounds and built an artificial lake to provide a parklike setting for the fair. Additional improvements were made to the interstate system leading into the downtown area, and new hotels were constructed in anticipation of the large crowds. Work also began on park facilities such as the Court of Flags, an area for hosting official ceremonies, an amphitheater known as the Tennessee State Pavilion, and the U.S. Pavilion. One of the most impressive new buildings was the Sunsphere, a steel tower with a five-story globe of reflective glass windows topped by a revolving restaurant and an observation deck. The Sunsphere quickly became the city's unofficial symbol and remains one of Knoxville's most recognizable landmarks.

On May 1, 1982, President Ronald Reagan officially opened the fair in Knoxville. Nearly eighty-eight thousand visitors attended opening day. By the end of the first week, more than 387,000 guests had visited the fair. Visitors enjoyed touring the exhibits of twenty-two nations, seven states, and more than fifty corporations. The European Community opened its first pavilion at a world exposition, allowing member states to feature individual exhibits within the pavilion. Many exhibits concentrated on the energy theme, such as U.S. Steel's exhibit of oil and gas drilling and exploration machinery and Mexico's focus on petroleum exports and energy development. One religious denomination, the Baptists, used the energy theme by highlighting "Spiritual Energy" in their exhibit.

Instead of focusing on energy, many countries chose to highlight cultural themes at the 1982 World's Fair. China, Peru, and Egypt hosted the most popular exhibits, all featuring cultural themes. At the Egyptian exhibit, for example, visitors viewed a collection of ancient treasures valued at more than $30 million. The popular Peruvian exhibit highlighted cultural artifacts, including a mummy that was unwrapped and studied at the fair.

Dozens of distinguished guests visited Knoxville during the fair's six months of operation, including the Crown Prince of Jordan, Hassan bin Talal. President Ferdinand Marcos of the Philippines toured his country's exhibit with his wife, Imelda, and comedian Bob Hope celebrated his seventy-ninth birthday at the fair. Entertainers ranging from actor/comedian Bill Cosby to country singer Johnny Cash performed at the fair, along with symphony orchestras and ballet companies hailing from countries and cities around the world.

The world's fair hosted numerous athletic exhibitions and events, including outdoor track championships, baseball and basketball tournaments, and an exhibition game played by members of the National Football League. The fair also sponsored a folklife festival featuring the arts, crafts, and culture of southern Appalachia. Special events honored participating nations on a daily basis, such as France National Day and Japan National Day.

By the time the fair closed on October 31, 1982, more than eleven million guests had visited the fairgrounds in East Tennessee. Attendance at Knoxville's fair exceeded the number of visitors at both the 1974 World's Fair in Spokane, Washington, and the 1962 World's Fair in Seattle, Washington.

The Filming of
Christy
• 1993 •

Surrounded by the majestic beauty of the Great Smoky
Mountains, the scenic village of Townsend provided the ideal
location for filming Catherine Marshall's best-selling novel,
Christy.

The story of *Christy* revolves around heroine Christy Rudd
Huddleston, a nineteen-year-old who leaves her home in
Asheville, North Carolina, during the winter of 1912 to teach at
a mission school in Cutter Gap, Tennessee. From the time of
the book's initial publication in 1967, *Christy* became an instant
bestseller. Readers eventually purchased more than eight million copies, enchanted by the story of Christy's determination,
courage, and faith to overcome hardships during her first year
of teaching in the Appalachian community. Facing such chal-
lenges as family feuds, poor medical care, and mountain su-
perstitions, Christy not only earns the trust and respect of the
community, but also learns to appreciate the mountain people
and their ways.

Author Catherine Marshall based the fictional story on the
actual experiences of her mother, Leonora Whitaker Wood,
who taught at a Presbyterian mission school in Del Rio, Tennessee, from 1910 to 1912. To research the story, Marshall visited the remote area of Del Rio in Cocke County and
interviewed local residents to gain insight into the customs of

the region during the early part of the twentieth century. Although Marshall sold the movie rights to the book in the 1960s, MGM shelved the project and never produced the film. After obtaining the movie rights in 1986, Hollywood producer Ken Wales accepted an offer from CBS to produce a television movie and series based on the book in 1993.

Wales and his crew considered filming the series at the actual site of Del Rio, but the Hollywood group soon discovered that the community's unpaved roads and remote mountain setting posed too many problems. Townsend's scenic vistas and valleys, however, offered a similar location with more accessibility for the production crew and cast. In preparation for the series, Wales leased a four-hundred-acre farm from a Townsend family and opened up the view of the surrounding mountains by clearing many of the pine trees from the land.

After studying photographs from the early 1900s, the show's production designer sketched out designs of buildings for the set and purchased antique furnishings from the region to use as props. Based on the designer's sketches, the set crew constructed twenty-two buildings on the farm in twenty-four days, including a mission house, a church, and several cabins. To give an aged, weathered look to the structures, the crew treated the lumber with chemicals. By the time filming began in September 1993, the Townsend farm had been transformed into a 1912-era Appalachian community.

Many local residents were hired as extras for the series, which starred actress Kellie Martin in the lead role of Christy. Veteran actors, including Tyne Daly and Tess Harper, also arrived and assumed starring roles in the series. Michael Rhodes, winner of five Emmy awards, directed the series. In addition to featuring the lush beauty of the Townsend farm, the producers filmed several scenes at local attractions, such as the Museum of Appalachia in nearby Norris, Tennessee.

Although author Catherine Marshall died more than a decade before her characters were brought to life on the screen, thirty-eight members of Marshall's family traveled to Townsend for a reunion during the filming of the series, including the author's son, Peter Marshall Jr. After delivering a Thanksgiving sermon in the small Baptist church, Peter Marshall and his family joined the cast and crew for a holiday dinner.

When *Christy* debuted on CBS on April 3, 1994, it received the highest ratings in six years for a series broadcast on an Easter Sunday. In all, twenty episodes of *Christy* were filmed in Townsend, including four segments that were originally telecast as two-hour specials. Six episodes aired in the spring of 1994, and a Thanksgiving special was broadcast on November 24, 1995. The remaining episodes were aired during the spring and summer of 1995. Reruns of the show on cable television continue to delight viewers, featuring the picturesque setting of Townsend as a backdrop for the enduring story of *Christy*.

A Potpourri of Tennessee Facts

- Tennessee is the thirty-fourth largest state in the nation, with a total area of 42,244 square miles, including inland waters. The greatest distance between the northern and southern borders is 115 miles; the greatest distance between the eastern and western borders is 480 miles.

- Clingman's Dome, located in Great Smoky Mountains National Park, is the highest point of elevation in Tennessee, at 6,643 feet (2,025 meters) above sea level.

- Shelby County, in the southwestern corner of the state, bordering the Mississippi River, is the lowest point of elevation in Tennessee, at 182 feet (55 meters) above sea level.

- The geographical center of Tennessee is located near Old Lascassas Pike, north of Murfreesboro.

- Tennessee has ninety-five counties.

- The capital of Tennessee is Nashville.

- The largest city in Tennessee is Memphis. In 2000, Memphis had a population of 650,100.

- The 2000 census concluded that Tennessee had a population of 5,689,283, making Tennessee the sixteenth most populated state in the nation.

- Tennessee was the sixteenth state to join the United States on June 1, 1796.

- Tennessee was the last state to withdraw from the Union on June 24, 1861, and it was the first Confederate state to be readmitted to the Union on July 24, 1866.

- The hottest temperature ever recorded in Tennessee was 133 degrees Fahrenheit at Perryville on August 9, 1940.

- The coldest temperature ever recorded in Tennessee was 32 degrees below zero in Mountain City on December 30, 1917.

- Tennessee has more than 3,800 documented caves.

- The "Lost Sea" in Sweetwater is the largest underground lake in the United States.

- Fall Creek Falls in Tennessee is the highest waterfall east of the Rocky Mountains, with a height of 256 feet.

- Tennessee has twenty major lakes and reservoirs and over 19,000 miles of warm and cold water streams.

- The Great Smoky Mountains National Park in Tennessee is the most visited national park in the United States.

- Three United States presidents have come from Tennessee: Andrew Jackson, James K. Polk, and Andrew Johnson.

- Tennessee is nicknamed the Volunteer State. The state motto is "Agriculture and Commerce."

- Tennessee has five official state songs: "My Homeland, Tennessee"; "When It's Iris Time in Tennessee"; "My Tennessee"; "Tennessee Waltz"; and "Rocky Top."

- The state poem is "Oh Tennessee, My Tennessee."

- The state folk dance is the square dance.

- The state flowers are the iris and the passionflower, and the state tree is the tulip poplar.

- The state bird is the mockingbird, and the state game bird is the bobwhite quail.

- The state insects are the ladybug and the firefly, the agricultural insect is the honeybee, and the state butterfly is the zebra swallowtail.

- The state commercial fish is the channel catfish, and the state game fish is the largemouth bass.

- The state wild animal is the raccoon.

- The state gem is the freshwater pearl, and the state rocks are agate and limestone.

Bibliography

Clemmer, Gregg S. *Valor in Gray: The Recipients of the Confederate Medal of Honor.* Staunton, VA: Hearthside Publishing Company, 1997.

Colman, Penny. *Spies! Women in the Civil War.* Cincinnati: Betterway Books, 1992.

DeBaryn, John, ed. *Dissipations at Uffington House, The Letters of Emily Hughes, Rugby, Tennessee, 1881–1887.* Memphis: Memphis State University Press, 1976.

Egerton, John. *Visions of Utopia.* Knoxville: University of Tennessee Press, 1977.

Embree, Elihu, with Ella P. Buchanan and John F. Nash. *The Emancipator.* Johnson City, TN: The Overmountain Press, 1995.

Ewing, James. *A Treasury of Tennessee Tales.* Nashville: Rutledge Hill Press, 1985.

————. *It Happened in Tennessee.* Nashville: Rutledge Hill Press, 1986.

Johnson, Leland, and Daniel Schaffer. *Oak Ridge National Laboratory: The First 50 Years.* Knoxville: University of Tennessee Press, 1994.

Larson, Edward J. *Summer for the Gods: The Scopes Trial and America's Continuing Debate over Science and Religion.* Boston: Harvard University Press, 1997.

Malone, Henry Thompson. *Cherokees of the Old South*. Athens: The University of Georgia Press, 1956.

Mitchamore, Pat. *A Tennessee Legend*. Nashville: Rutledge Hill Press, 1992.

Patrick, Jean L. S. *The Girl Who Struck Out Babe Ruth*. Minneapolis: Carolrhoda Books, 2000.

Price, Charles Edwin. *The Day They Hung the Elephant*. Johnson City, TN: The Overmountain Press, 1992.

Sawyer, Susan. *More Than Petticoats: Remarkable Tennessee Women*. Helena, MT: Falcon Publishing, 2000.

Ward, Geoffrey C., with Ric Burns and Ken Burns. *The Civil War: An Illustrated History*. New York: Alfred A. Knopf, 1991.

Wheeler, Marjorie Spruill, ed. *Votes for Women: The Women Suffrage Movement in Tennessee, the South, and the Nation*. Knoxville: University of Tennessee Press, 1995.

Whiteaker, Larry H., and W. Calvin Dickinson. *Tennessee: State of the Nation*. New York: American Heritage, 1998.

Wilson, John. *Chattanooga's Story*. Chattanooga, TN: Chattanooga News-Free Press, 1980.

Yellin, Carol Lynn, and Janann Sherman. *The Perfect 36: Tennessee Delivers Woman Suffrage*. Memphis: Vote 70, 1998.

Index

About the Author

Susan Sawyer enjoys exploring the past and writing about historical topics. History serves as the centerpiece for many of her writings, taking the form of both fact and fiction. Drawing upon her fascination with the history of her native South, Susan is the author of fourteen books, including Globe Pequot's *More than Petticoats: Remarkable Tennessee Women.*

A graduate of the University of Tennessee, Susan worked as a magazine editor and communications consultant before establishing a career as a freelance writer and published author. Today, she writes from her home in Tennessee, where she lives with her husband, Ron, and miniature schnauzer, Maxwell Smart Sawyer.